Gramps

by

Norman Sheridan Stafford

Library of Congress Control Number: 2003102026

ISBN 1-930648-58-8

Published in conjunction with

Goose River Press
3400 Friendship Road
Waldoboro ME 04572

Edited by:
Norma Jean Hissong

Cover by:
Chris Pugh
Dawna Jean Holloway

Contents

Sixty-two years of action and thought in 159 pages...

To

my God, my country, my wife, my eight children, my ten grandchildren...

and

my long-deceased diabetic brother John who followed me one weekend of busy catering and remarked,

"Boy, the day I beat you was the day I learned to sign the paychecks on the back instead of the front."

Preface

This started to be a story about John Doe, but the I, me, my, that he has become, was necessary because the story is more factual than anyone would have bothered to dream up.

I've left most of the sex, and the bulk of the language of the day out, in hopes that a lot of kids will read it. I also hope some who are worried about their future get more worried, and do something to create a turnabout.

When I started to clean up the mess of stuff that had accumulated in my basement through the years - while I'd been in and out of the hospital - I recalled telling one of our daughters that I would write that book I'd always dreamed of, talked about.

I knew the odds were about a thousand to one against getting it published, and way more than that against getting it read, appreciated, or paid for.

Books that sell are about people who did something - went to jail; made headlines for years; came up with some far-out idea for changing the rules of conduct, or a new theory of what was or might be. The other 220 million people who populate the nation are, supposedly, not worth writing about.

There is a chance, though, of making this one John Doe worthy of note. A lot of people didn't do as many different things as I did, or make as many notes about them.

Maybe it'll work if I make a promise that everything really happened - although maybe not exactly as I record it. Then I'll ask permission from the reader to skip around while covering a lot of ground. I'll also have to state, early on, that the real reason for writing the thing - besides the promise to my daughter - is to explain why I get upset over politicians more often than I ignore them, and why I won't buy their rhetoric.

That'll give the dyed-in-the-wool Drinan, O'Neil, Kennedy type a chance to save their time and money. On the other hand, it might make some of them curious enough to want to follow the evolution of such a character.

I've got to realize that I was a lot sharper forty years ago and could fit words together better then too. I've always done things in a half-vast sort of way. As a matter of fact, forty years ago I was sure I could do anything and everything and thought I already had.

Of course I didn't do them all perfectly, even then.

Foreward

by

Norma Jean Hissong

Recently, at my daughter's, I spotted the book my father wrote (finished in 1978). Father-O had done the whole book on a typewriter, no personal word processors back then.

After having helped many hospice patients write their stories, I realized I couldn't remember what my father had written. I borrowed the book from Dawna, and went through it, wondering as I did if it could possibly be for the first time. The stories all seemed new. They were interesting and entertaining.

Father-O had gone through the finished project and added hand written notes before he made comb-bound copies for everyone. I decided to keyboard the book into a computer file - incorporating his hand written notes and corrections, add some photos, then reprint it for his intended audience, his grandchildren.

Father-O's book is about growing up during the depression, and working his way through college. It's about meeting Mom, and the time he spent in the Navy during the Second World War. He tells us what he did to support his large family, but it's not full of stories about that large family as we'd expected when he kept threatening to write a book. He shares with us his attitudes about business and politics. Though we may not learn a lot about that family, we learn where they came from, and perhaps why they think the way they do.

In the process of putting this book together I've read it a number of times and enjoy it more each time I read it. I've wondered how I could have blown it off years ago just because it wasn't about us.

While assembling Father-O's work, I've sometimes found myself overwhelmed with sadness to think that he poured his heart into this project and, to the best of my knowledge, never got any positive feedback. But, most of all, I've loved doing this project and hope Father-O's looking down, accepting the long overdue accolades that ring out as I read. I hope the rest of you enjoy **Gramps** as much as I have.

Musings

Now I'm looking back through the rear view mirror of a big truck at the mess I'd just left on a Kansas highway.

Two cross-country gypsy truckers had picked me up when I was hitchhiking from Texas to a new job in Garden City, Kansas.

They'd stopped at the Oklahoma border and declared their cargo as "general" when they entered the dry state of Kansas. During this stop they asked me if I'd ever driven a truck and, after an affirmative answer, decided that one of them should get on top of the load and take a little nap while I took the wheel. The owner climbed up and took his shoes off to get a good rest.

These two had been driving steady for three days, and the other fellow soon dozed off in the cab - after it had become obvious to him that I knew how to get started, shift gears, etc. like the veteran driver I'd proclaimed to be. It was at just about that time that the highway curved - which it does some places, even in Kansas. I slowed down, but not enough. The tractor made the turn all right but the trailer tipped sidewise on the middle of the road. The truck's owner, hopping around barefooted among all those hundreds of cases of broken, illicit, foaming beer bottles, in search of his shoes, is one of those pictures that comes clearly back to mind but has little to do with the story.

The trucker's second thought was to get me out of the picture so the insurance man wouldn't know that an unlicensed, inexperienced kid had been at the wheel. He flagged down the next truck and sent me on my way.

At my destination, where I'd been hired by an older brother who was fresh out of college, I took over as Intertype operator. I'd never seen an Intertype before.

Because the dust storms had just hit, it had been necessary to tape up every crack around every window and door to keep the fine powdery dust from ruining the machinery. The streetlights burned all day but nothing was visible.

The owner, whose nickname of "Boozie" was well earned, was off somewhere writing checks, which my brother was frantically trying to cover each day. Boozie didn't return for two weeks so there was no way to know what my pay was. On his return he studied the production of this newly hired kid - along with his bank balance - and decided that, on piecework from this unfamiliar and dust covered machine, $8.00 a week would be "about right."

Again, nothing to do with this story but to add a little notoriety to it, a sidelight should be recorded.

On a Sunday we brothers went a few miles out in the country to visit some distant cousins on their farm. They were the family who found fame - but not fortune - by being killed "In Cold Blood" some years later. If Mr. Capote had not made a best seller out of their misfortune, they would have continued to be just a small portion of the 220 million who get their names in the paper only at birth, on their marriage, and at their demise.

That was the twenty-first of the twenty-two jobs I had between high school and college, but we'll get back to those and the next one later.

The reader should bear in mind that these jobs were all available in the depths of the depression - between June of 1933 and December of 1935.

Now it would be prudent, it seems, to skip up to whatever happened to the Southwestern University Class of '39?

A quick check of the old yearbook, dug out of a dusty cupboard, showed there weren't enough members in the class to tell much. It'd have to be like a modern pollster's production. Even then it couldn't be accurate as a microcosm. At least 99 percent were Methodists. All lived in Texas. All were white. About two-thirds were male. Nearly half were "townies" - who missed half the fun of going to college by not living on campus. About 20 percent had majored in pure science with the intention of post-graduate study. Over half of the girls had planned on teaching careers of one sort or another - in case they didn't get married first.

Only a couple showed any intent to become ministers - even though this was a Methodist College and a large part of the student body was made up of tuition-exempt ministers' kids who, generally speaking, were the biggest hell-raisers.

3

The other 28 percent majored in business administration for various reasons. I made no bones about the reason for my choice. It was the only way I could figure to get through. I was so busy working to pay the bills that I didn't have time to read the books I would have been required to buy and study in the science department; and I had no talent for the fine arts.

––––––––––

Since graduation day in June, 1939 I've seen only two of the 51 who donned their caps and gowns in that little central Texas town.

At the time, one was driving a milk truck in Houston. The other, who'd attended on a football scholarship, was repossessing cars for a finance company, also in Houston. He had a special deal with them; every time he got beat up they would buy him another suit (for $19.95). I had the best job of the lot. I was assistant editor, chief reporter, and production manager for an East Texas newspaper - at $25 per week.

The obvious manner in which this jumps around is partly caused by an unconscious effort to make sure it doesn't get beyond the state of the promise I made to my daughter. If it really came out with a message and established the fact that we have practically entered the oft predicted negative Utopia - and that it isn't too late yet to avoid the inevitable - it might succeed and become a moneymaker.

Then my problems would start all over again. My only problem now is to pass the time between morning and evening without: (1) feeling that it was completely wasted, (2) being too productive, or (3) expending too much physical energy. The first would be against my inbred nature; the second would be against the law; and the third would be against doctor's orders.

In other words I'm one of those millions who has worked himself up to the public trough as physically disabled.

My wife is a schoolteacher. Our house is almost paid for. The last of the brood is nearing the end of college. If I don't rock the boat, and if inflation doesn't get too rampant, I'm "all set." This seems to be the modern goal - a firm slot at the trough where sustenance can be obtained.

The daily television blurbs (each making certain to repeat what the other said lest they be accused of being scooped), and the papers and news magazines (which do the same) all record the unusual and often bizarre tales of how someone figured out a way to beat the system and get a little cake and ice cream. Few of the 220 million though, get into this. Also frequently reported is some new way in which the government - local, state, federal - has figured how to take a little more from the worker and give a little more to the non-worker.

This is done on the theory that there are more non-workers - including, of course, bureaucrats and other government drones - who will actually go down and vote, than there are workers who produce the product that makes the contents of the trough.

Of course the workers get up to the trough too, but they mostly have to take seconds. Hundreds of thousands of them labor all day at jobs that would be unacceptable to those who are first in line and sure of a full portion.

I got to thinking of the things I've seen in real estate the past few years. There's no need to go into elaborate detail because everyone knows of the tremendous waste that goes into the design and construction of "projects" financed with public money. The results of most of them are far beyond the dream of the ordinary worker, and the cost, (not the rent) far beyond what he could pay. (Here, it must be said, the elderly who had enough political clout to work their way into these projects, have generally kept them in good condition.)

Other housing projects, though, populated by those who had the clout to get on general welfare - or ADC or some other program that entitles them to move in - start to deteriorate on the first day. Soon they are a blight on the entire neighborhood - a shame to those in modest homes around them who, besides paying for them, are watching them make the value of their own property deteriorate. It's the old saw, "You can take the people out of the slum, but you can't take the slum out of the people."

This message isn't new - it was in a play well over 20 years ago.

HUD keeps spending billions of dollars though - because these are the people who get out to vote. If they didn't vote (and on the proper side), they wouldn't have gotten the apartment in the first place.

Let's take to the microcosm approach again. Everybody knows the hopes and the problems of the peanut man.

Take the little suburban city, ten miles from Boston, where I finally landed some eight years ago.

Right away I felt the coolness.

I'd stumbled across the perfect example of the fact that the Great American Dream, as dreamed by FDR and his successors, simply won't work...<u>People don't want to be homogenized</u>.

We got a call from the folks across the street from the house we'd just bought. The message from this Jewish couple - who were selling and moving to Winchester - was this: "Don't you realize you're moving into an Irish ghetto?"

I had never heard of one, didn't know one existed - and couldn't have cared less.

It's interesting to note, though, in the second edition of *Massachusetts - A Guide to the Pilgrim State*, copyright by Houghton Mifflin Company in 1971, and edited by Ray Bearse (but originally written during the depression as part of a WPA project), there is this verbatim comment concerning Woburn. "Roman Catholic and Greek Orthodox groups broke down the once Congregational Homogeneity - much to the distress of established citizens." Concerning Winchester, the same guide notes that it was "settled in 1640 and incorporated in 1850...after having been successively called Woburn Gates, South Woburn and Black Horse Village." Wilmington and Burlington (other abutting suburbs) had seceded earlier.

My wife, whose genealogy shows her ancestors representing Woburn in both the Civil and the Revolutionary wars, thought nothing of it.

She does remember, though, that her great grandfather kept his GAR post running all by himself while, across the street, the last survivor of the Irish Post kept his running also.

Anyway let's get back to why we were moving from Winchester to Woburn. We were possibly the first to have ever done so.

When the last of our eight children to attend the public schools started first grade it didn't make sense to Mrs. Stafford to "sit around and drink coffee with the neighbors for the next forty years." She went back to school, and at the twenty-fifth anniversary of her graduation from Tufts, she donned cap and gown to accept her hard-earned Master's Degree and Teacher's Certificate.

It was only then, when she began job-hunting, that she started to realize the difference between

Burbank Post of the GAR, Woburn, MA
WIlliam C C Colgate 2nd to right of big man in front.

9

school systems. There was a definite feeling she should not teach in the Winchester system because of her long years of association with so many of the parents. The quickest and easiest alternative was to apply in Woburn - where the pay was less but where, with a Master's degree, she was quickly accepted.

Then there was the story of Uncle John's green houses and the fact it had been suggested I might find a customer for them.

They just filled the bill as the new location for the Cadillac agency, which had to move, and a tentative deal was quickly made. Right next door to them was the proper house for us - much smaller than the one we no longer needed because five of our brood had already left the roost.

It was on a state highway, had a nice driveway, a big old barn, a grape arbor, what was left of an old apple orchard and, it had been for sale for several months.

A quick study of the zoning law showed that use of this for a real estate office would be perfectly acceptable without asking anyone. However, a public hearing would be necessary before Uncle John's green houses could be replaced by the Cadillac man.

I, of course, had to make this "permission for business use" a condition of the sale. My first move was to call the self-appointed "West Side Guardian" who published a monthly newsletter for the area - to arrange to discuss the move with her. The answer was a simple and direct shocker.

"It won't do you any good to talk to me because whatever you're in favor of, I'm against."

That's the way we still get along nine years later. I've won about ten of our heated battles and she's won two. My ten have helped the city. Her two have hurt. She was on the Board of Aldermen and I wasn't. Now she's out.

It took three weeks for the Cadillac man to get City Council approval and over two years to get final approval through the courts because of the West Side Guardian.

Again though, that's a whole different story and we want to keep this brief.

———————

11

The War Years

My story will, of course, have to include some sea stories. Every old timer who ever wore a uniform had to have some of them. Some, more or less, found one spot but here again, I ran the spectrum. I hit all four kinds of Navy. Each had a different degree of homogeneity

(1) The trade school type of prewar Navy as it was winding down.

(2) The new construction Navy as it was getting into full swing.

(3) The fast fleet operational Navy - where I won nine battle stars and a Presidential unit citation without ever seeing an enemy - (except one dead one).

(4) The back-up Navy where, if I'd been so inclined and less busy, I could have written *The Caine Mutiny* and *Tales of the South Pacific* - both from facts and with embellishments.

A Chronicle of this type - written nearly forty years after the fact certainly has no business going into detail on all these subjects, but little vignettes of the passing scene should be helpful to anyone who wants to try to understand the product about which this is being written.

I'd been turned down by the Army Air Force after a three-day physical exam came up with the fact that I had a scar on my eardrum, the result of an inner ear infection during my youth. The doctor explained, "The severe strain of a power dive might rupture the eardrum; then we'll not only lose the aircraft but all the money we spent in training you."

The fact that I had a college degree ruled me out of the normal draft process. The only opening at the time, in the Navy officer-training program, was in a school for engineering duty. I didn't qualify for this because I didn't have the required mathematics background. I was, therefore, sworn in as an "apprentice seaman on inactive duty, without pay, awaiting orders," and had been in that status six months when the attack on Pearl Harbor came.

Soon I was ordered to report to Northwestern University (downtown campus) in Chicago for training as a deck officer. There were one thousand recent college graduates from all over the land who were thoroughly tested, both physically and mentally, for this program, which was quickly dubbed the "ninety-day wonders" - although it was really a four-month program. The first month was spent in basic physical conditioning, dental repairs, and uniform outfitting. Celluloid collars were no longer required, but detachable collars still were. Each one was personally fitted at several stages of the construction of tailor-made uniforms. The next ninety days were spent in digesting every military textbook from Annapolis - except those on engineering.

The entire group was required to learn to navigate as Bowditch had done, with spherical trigonometry. The only practical way to do this was from tables that had been painstakingly developed during the depression by thousands of unemployed mathematicians. The reason for learning the old way was simply "you might run across some old sea dog who'll look down his nose at you if you only learned the short cuts."

Anyone who was not learning "up to snuff" was "hung on the tree" and made to stay in and study all weekend while the others had limited "liberty." Repeated infractions meant you were out - and about 20 percent fell by the wayside, to be transferred to an enlisted men' "boot camp."

We were in the process of becoming "gentlemen by Act of Congress" and would, by virtue of our engraved calling cards, be welcome as guests in any club in the civilized world. Part of this training, of course, required a daily cocktail hour before dinner, but we were restricted to a small neighborhood each day. No one who attended will ever forget Mme. Galli and the beautiful and bounteous trays of hors d'oeuvres, which went down with her below-cost drinks. On weekend liberties we were allowed to wander a little farther, and I fondly remember a fellow who'd gone to school in Cambridge (which I thought meant England), who took all 16 of his roommates to his father's club and signed the chit himself.

Many debutante types (I remember, particularly, one who said her mother made her wear a chastity girdle) arranged parties on the weekend.

There was a graduation ball at the Edgewater Beach Hotel, to which I had planned to escort a young lady by way of streetcar. Instead her uncle sent a chauffeured Rolls Royce.

There was the inevitable questionnaire as to what sort of duty each would prefer - first, second, and third choices. Alternatives were many: armed guard on merchant ships, bomb disposal school, P. T. boats, destroyers, cargo ships, "the fleet" (which was by then almost nonexistent), flight training, remaining there as an instructor, Navy intelligence, communication, etc.

It was a red-letter day when the assignments were posted. Nearly everyone got something he hadn't requested. The one that made the most sense, we all agreed, was the fellow from Cambridge who'd spent all his life around small boats and yachts and was assigned to P. T. boats.

I (and twelve others) was assigned to the battleship Colorado, the only "fleet" between there and Guadalcanal, and given orders to proceed to join her at Long Beach.

(See:www.historycentral.com/Navy/battle/Colarado.html -misspelling necessary- and www.navsource.org/archives/01/45.htm)

We saluted the quarterdeck in prescribed fashion and were immediately escorted to meet the commanding officer, then led to the spacious quarters of the executive officer for indoctrination and assignment. His opening remarks still ring in my ears.

"Every ship in the Navy needs one son of a bitch to keep her going and before you've been here five minutes you'll know that's me. You all think you've learned a lot but I'll show you that you don't know anything."

The new "boots" were then lined up alphabetically and assigned to divisions. The last two (I and another) were to report to the engineering officer. When we reminded the exec that we'd been trained for deck duty only, he simply waved that aside and said, "We'll train you."

The engineering officer took us on a quick tour of the vitals of this outmoded behemoth - the rooms, surrounded by sixteen-inch armor plate, were made airtight during battle conditions. He handed us a sheaf of "Standing Orders of the Engineering Officer" and a mail-order type course in basic marine engineering, which each of us was to study. We were to stand watches four hours on and eight hours off and learn all this material during the off time.

When we got underway, my watch station was on a leather cushion. The air-conditioned Main Control Room was where two chief electricians' mates actually controlled the movements of the monster with two little toggles - each of which could be moved by one finger.

There was an instrument board about ten by forty feet, which had hundreds of dials, and a big bank of intercom telephones but no actual sound or motion such as you might expect at the center of such a huge lot of machinery.

As fourth junior officer of the watch, without a seat to sit on, I was given a quick briefing of the overall operation, then told to wander around at random - through the various fire rooms, engine rooms, propeller shaft alleys, steering rooms, evaporator rooms, and machine shops that made up the domain of the chief engineer. My battle station was one of the engine rooms - where a turbine driven generator made power for a huge electric motor that turned the screw and, teamed with the others, could drive this monster through the water at about half the speed of the ships of the "modern" Navy, which was each day becoming more nonexistent.

When we were well clear of the harbor - bound for Pearl Harbor - a "general quarters" was sounded, and practice firing commenced. When the blast of those sixteen-inch guns reverberated through the ventilation system, I was reminded of the Army doctor back at San Antonio and wondered how much worse the pressure on the eardrums from a power dive might be.

On arrival at Pearl Harbor, in June of 1942, a strange hush fell over everyone. The devastation we saw was so much more than had been expected. Few ships had been there since, and very little cleanup or rehabilitation had been accomplished.

As my designated watch lined up for the first "liberty," I saluted the department head in the prescribed fashion and requested "Permission to go ashore, Sir?"

Back came the question, "Are your study assignments up to date, Sir?"

"No, Sir."

"Stay aboard, Sir."

The stay there was brief, and the ship headed for the Fiji Islands - while still feverishly in the process of "stripping ship for action." Decades of paint were chipped off the bulkheads. Battleship linoleum was discarded. Soon the "one thin coat" of fire resistant paint was discovered to be useless as a rust inhibitor, and the process of building up the paint started all over again.

Upon arrival in Fiji, it was determined we'd been too late to be of any real help in the fighting at Guadalcanal. The best bet was to get this monster into the safe harbor at Nandi, close the submarine nets behind her, and let her ride in the moorage until some of the new Navy could become a reality.

In her role as a training ship, she had been, of course, greatly over-manned. The junior officers' wardroom had bunks welded to the bulkheads. These had to be folded up out of the way before the tables could be set for breakfast, and the possibilities of "sack time" - which was to later become a favorite occupation - was out of the question.

Aside from the watches and the training study courses, the only diversion was censoring mail and occasional trips to the beach (where the Fiji home guard were feverishly marching up and down and creating gun emplacements against the possibility of invasion). The mail censoring was a real shocker. I couldn't believe so many of America's finest were so illiterate. A typical letter home was "Hi, Maw. The chow's lousy. G'bye."

It was hard to realize there was a war going on and all this equipment and manpower was sitting here so useless. Finally the big day came. The word spread through the ship like wildfire. There was to be a major transfer of personnel back to the States "on or about December 20" for duty in connection with the construction and fitting out of new ships. My orders were to a heavy cruiser being built in Boston. "On or about" meant 20 days either way so it seemed only typical of what had become known as the "trade school mentality" that most detachment orders called for December 26. Those for officers allowed air transportation "if available."

I made my way by train to Houston where I got a chance to say hello to "the girl I'd left behind," my old boss, my parents and brothers and sisters (I was the only one of the eight brothers and sisters who had been able to don a uniform). I barely made it to Boston before the ten days ran out.

The next six months could keep a soap opera going for years, but we'll have to condense it here so we can get sixty years into a short enough volume that my grandchildren might want to read it. A few things must be recorded, though.

There was the first reaction when I turned that Fiji suntan into the wind, which blew from the South-east around the Fargo Building in South Boston, for the first time: "If the pilgrim fathers had discovered Texas, there'd be nobody here but Eskimos!"

The Bachelor Officers' Quarters in this big, old converted wool warehouse were full, so the new arrivals were steered to furnished rooms on Commonwealth Avenue - where the only heat source was folded-up newspapers to burn in the fireplace. In a search for better quarters the dowdy appearance and high rent of what was available appalled us.

My buddy - Pete Bonan - said, "When this war is over, we will do something about this!"

We soon found paradise. A wing (which had formerly been maids' quarters and didn't have private baths) of the Copley Plaza Hotel had just been done over for the use of Bachelor Officers. Red carpets, slippers, white bathrobes, and four beds to the room were all new. The rent, just under the allowance made by the Government, allowed us to live in one of the city's finest hotels cheaper than in the old converted wool warehouse to which we reported for duty each morning.

"Duty" was slow to develop. The ship was far from finished as the crew slowly assembled from every walk of life. The nucleus was those with some real experience who had lost their ships at Pearl Harbor, Midway, or the South Pacific. The group from the Colorado and other such ships tried to help them, and to give some basic information to the real "boots," who were now streaming out of Great Lakes and similar swearing in and outfitting centers. Again it was amazing to discover how ignorant they were - in general. Scores of five, ten and fifteen per cent were routine on the simplest sort of tests made from study books that had been written for this type of student.

An essential part of the weekly routine was to gather all hands and read to them "The Rocks and Shoals," which was the code of military justice.

Scolley Square - home of the Crawford House, the Old Howard, the Half Dollar Bar and dozens of lesser joints - was declared out of bounds to officers and was well policed by the MPs. Still there were lots of young bluejackets who found it impossible to keep their noses clean, and court martial was routine.

The wearers of the gold braid, the Gentlemen by Act of Congress, stumbled a few times too.

There were, for instance, the two young lawyers who were having a drink together at the Merry-go Round when they were joined by a couple of young ladies. After about three refills they asked for the check, left their share, and excused themselves. The dumbfounded waiter called his boss, who called the shore patrol, who picked up the two young officers and returned them to the "ship." The skipper gave them the alternative of paying for the young ladies' drinks or being restricted to quarters for a week. The lawyers stuck to the principle - they hadn't invited any company - and stayed aboard for a week. I've often wondered what's happened to them and their principles by now.

There was another group of "young turks" who didn't like having the famous Sally Keith (queen of the tassels) placed "off limits" to them. They, through her manager, invited her to dinner in the Wardroom aboard ship. I can still hear the shouting from the crew when Sally made her grand walk up the gangway, saluted the quarterdeck and headed for the Officers' Quarters.

There was the young lady from Chicago, with the Rolls Royce, who heard I was in Boston and called to invite me to the hockey game. She arrived with her mother and finally got around to asking me when I was going to get married. My only practical answer was "Some time when the war is over." Her immediate retort was, "You mean I can tell Mother we're engaged?" I was sort of in a box.

A few days later Joan Roberts, whom I'd met in San Francisco some months before, looked me up with a ticket to the opening of a new musical *Away We Go* and a request I sit with her after the show and meet the cast while they waited for the reviews. Such negative reviews as "Away will go all the customers..." made them ecstatic. To be panned in Boston was a sure sign of success to show people. When it opened in New York as *Oklahoma!*, the cast was proven to have been right, and the Boston panners wrong.

Now we must digress again. There was Lieutenant Axsel, who wore the gold braid but hadn't yet discovered he was a "gentleman by act of congress."

He had, through a period of twenty years in the regular navy, worked up to chief gunner's mate and had finally been commissioned in another of the many programs by which the expanding navy was being manned.

Axsel, a mammoth North Carolinian, with his shiny new braid, had appeared in our private floor of one of Boston's finest hostelry's about two weeks before. He'd whistled at the appointments and quickly came out with the comment, "Think of all the weeks I wasted around the Touraine before I discovered that the Costly Pleasure was where I belonged."

He still spent a lot of time at the Touraine studying the field and handing out his number to the more likely looking chicks with an admonition such as "Call me at my hotel Tuesday." The number of calls he got was amazing. I saw him in the lobby one midnight and asked him what he was doing out of bed. His quick reply was, "I have finally found my true love — I so love her that I got dressed and brought her down to the taxi."

Now back to *Oklahoma!* This nice little leading lady, who had stars in her eyes—but no idea as to how soon stardom would hit, had suggested that we meet the next evening for a light supper—after I got away from the office and before her performance. She said she knew of a cute little place, which she would show me.

The next morning, at mess in the Officers' Club of the Fargo Building, an apparition appeared.

It was the first WAVE officer any of us had ever seen. She walked, all alone, into this room full of two hundred young male officers. I was about twelfth in line behind Axsel to greet her and ask her to my table. Somehow, she came with me.

It was almost eight bells and time to "be aboard" so there was little time for food—let alone conversation. We decided to meet after five o'clock and go to some quiet little place to get better acquainted. I, of course, was then faced with calling the Colonial and leaving a message that I couldn't make the date with Joan Roberts.

The lonesome WAVE and I met as planned. She suggested we go to an out-of-the-way little place on Beacon Street.

There, two tables away, Joan Roberts and Alfred Drake were just being seated.

———————

Jean Gray Colgate

This first short meeting between me, and the future Mrs. Stafford, seemed to make each of us more certain than before that we'd been made for each other. She loved three cities — three of the five I knew anything about. She'd been through Denver, many times, on her way to Mills College in Oakland — across the Bay from San Francisco — and was a dyed in the wool Yankee who had finished college at Tufts University. I'd spent fifteen years in the Denver area, where I was born, so little time in Houston or Chicago that I barely knew them, but enough in San Francisco and Boston to have created a real soft spot for either or both.

She'd been assigned to the Fargo Building temporarily, after receiving, at Smith College, basic officer training similar to what I got at Northwestern. She was now awaiting the opening of a course in supply, at Radcliffe. I was leaving in three days for a training course in fire fighting, at Norfolk, VA. It might well have been one of those cases like ships that pass in the night — and only send signals to each other. We corresponded, though.

On my return from Virginia a call to my bride-to-be at Radcliffe brought instructions on how to find my way to that elusive Cambridge subway.

27

Norman & Jean on the bank of the Charles River

We learned how it was to lie on the banks of the Charles in full uniform and dream about what it would be like if only I didn't have to go to sea and she hadn't pledged not to marry.

She couldn't get out after dinner, and I was getting more and more snowed under with detail as the ship came nearer to completion. This went on for weeks.

Finally in mid-May came word that the Bureau of Personnel would allow WAVE officers to marry after completion of their formal training — in other words on graduation from Radcliffe. That would be a week before our new ship would make her trial run to the Caribbean.

The wedding date was set for June 9, 1943 — about six months since I'd arrived from the Fiji Islands, and about two months before our ship would head for a serious stab at the enemies who had so disrupted the country. Jean took me out to meet her father (Arthur), stepmother (Alyce), sister (Sally), and Great Aunt Eula - each of whom, although only another of the 220 million, deserves a book. Aunt Eula, daughter of the last Civil War veteran in Woburn, quizzed this Texan from Colorado at considerable length before giving the family stamp of approval. I, in turn, wrote my folks in Texas with an explanation that my bride-to-be had been sufficiently deprovincialized by having spent two years on the West Coast.

The minister at the Methodist church, where Jean had spent all the years of her youth, admonished us not to "smell up my church with booze like the last Navy wedding did." We arranged for punch and cookies in the church basement so we could get away from the reception in time to catch a commuter train to a "Honeymoon Hotel" in Swampscott — a suburb about ten miles away. We each arranged for a group of "shipmates" to serve as the bridal party, and Jean's father - the first grandfather in the nation to volunteer on Dec. 8, now a first-class ship's cook at the Fargo Building - gave the bride away.

The Boston Globe photographed the group and dutifully recorded that "Colgate stood unabashed midst all the gold braid."

Wedding announcements were sent rather than the customary invitations. The three girls I was more or less engaged to each got one. Probably the fellow whose diamond Jean had been wearing got one too.

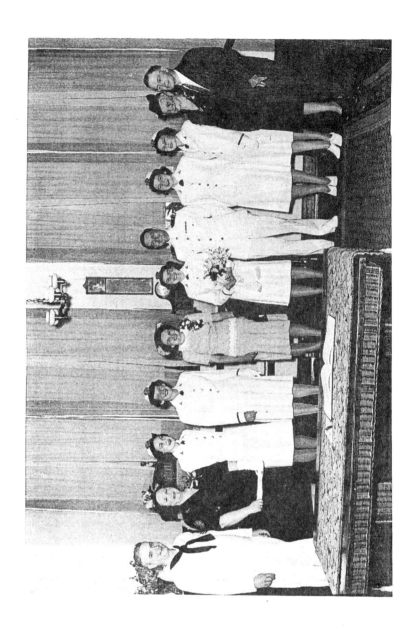

Arthur & Alyce Colgate on the left, Sally (Colgate) Stonehouse next to Jean (Colgate) & Norman Stafford, Elsie & Irvin Stafford on the right.

The shakedown cruise to Trinidad was far from smooth or routine — as were the training drills, which were a part of it. There was plenty to be done in a hurry when the Big B — second of her class — came back into Boston Naval Shipyard for her post-shake-down availability.

My first thought on docking was, of course, "Where's Jean?" It turned out that her orders had been changed and she'd been assigned to the section base at Portland, Maine — about four hours away by train. Love conquers all, and I commuted, arriving in Portland at ten and catching a milk train back four hours later.

Finally came the inevitable time when I was just too tired. So my wife decided to take the train down to see me. I got a hotel room and left word for a call, which would give me plenty of time to meet the train, then laid down for a little nap.

Of course you guessed.

The call didn't come and the nap continued.

The new bride, unmet at the station, called her father after calling every hotel she could think of. He, being the type that he was, consoled her with the suggestion her new husband had probably found someone more attractive.

The inevitable day came when the ship was considered ready for action and headed for the Panama Canal and the ever-growing fleet.

My men in the machine shop gave me a souvenir made from the base of a five-inch shell casing and inscribed "First round fired from the guns of the USS Baltimore at Makin Island November 20, 1943." This was about eleven months after I'd arrived for duty aboard a nearly completed ship.

(See: http://www.historycentral.com/Navy/cruiser/ Baltimore2.html and www.navsource.org/archives/09/130105.htm)

Our first engagement was around Baker Island right near Pearl Harbor, when some Jap planes attacked and were being fought off by the destroyer screen and the Combat Air Patrol.

One plane broke through all the surrounding flak and got within easy range of the untried gunners of the new addition to the fleet. Axsel, who with his still shiny gold braid, was supposed to stand back and give orders, played the wrong role. After the first few rounds from his 40-MM gun missed their mark, he grabbed the controls from the gunner's mate and fired as he had been trained to do for twenty years. Bulls eye! Then it was discovered that the target was one of our own planes that, against all orders, had penetrated the screen while in mad pursuit of a Jap. The pilot, though picked up, was a little peeved.

Axsel was ordered to paint an American flag on his gun mount.

The softening up of Makin Island by bombers and strafing aircraft and hours of constant bombardment from every cruiser and battleship (including my old home the Colorado) available practically defoliated the island. It seemed impossible that anything, let alone any human being, could still be alive there.

Then the assault troops headed ashore. An old sunken hulk - which had been noted on the charts as a hazard to navigation - turned out to be a literal fortress which started firing at the assault troops, from behind, after they had carefully skirted it. Then the beach came alive with little yellow men who had been hunched in pillboxes and caves and palm lined dugouts. The losses to our troops were overwhelmingly severe as compared to estimates.

Everything had been fun and games for a year or so. Now the mood changed.

All this activity and high speed maneuvering had shown serious mechanical deficiencies in the Big B. Attempts had been made at Boston, at Norfolk, at San Francisco and again at Pearl Harbor to correct a deficiency in the meshing, which caused the huge herringbone reduction gears to overheat.

Badly as the ship was needed, it was decided to send her back to San Francisco to get this major problem corrected.

I was able to arrange for my wife to come out to the City by the Golden Gate and spent several more weeks in fond farewells - this time to the lady who would be mother of our son in June.

Jean Colgate Stafford

We went to the zoo and took her picture standing beside an elephant.

The Naval Bureau of Personnel continued to be busy trying to man new ships with sprinklings of experienced people and making the most of what they had. My orders came through to join the aircraft carrier Belleau Wood at Espirito Santo, (via a long and hazardous flight in a Navy DC 3. A flat tire on takeoff, poor braking on a too-short runway at a refueling stop, and navigational problems all entered in to making it a hair-raiser I'll long remember.) I was assigned as Boiler Division, and Fueling and Stability Officer, duties with which I had had minimal experience, but which could be handled by anyone who could read and was willing to try. *The Manual of Engineering Instructions* - emphasized by instruction plates at every station and supplemented by standing orders of the engineering officer, along with a "log room" full of files, blue prints, and walls covered by piping and compartment diagrams, (most all a legacy from the peacetime Navy) - was the only thing that made this rapid expansion possible.

Some things couldn't be covered, though.

After several non-eventful "fueling at sea" operations, I was relieved from my post one morning for a cup of coffee by a new assistant who had just reported for duty.

This was simply coincidence. It would have happened to me, or anyone.

Acting as fueling officer this new "boot ensign" was standing at the door of the hanger deck with his TBS (talk between ships) phones ready to tell the tanker when he wanted it to stop pumping, to switch tanks. A sudden lurch of the seas between the two ships put too much pressure on this huge 8-inch rubber oil hose, which was nearly cut it in two on the sharp edge of the hangar deck. The full force of the high-pressure fuel oil hit the "talker" square in the face so that it was impossible for him to say a word about stopping the pumps. During the several minutes of total confusion that followed - before the word was relayed by other means - thousands of gallons of fuel oil sprayed the aircraft spare parts hung on the bulkheads of the hangar deck, and ran to the deck, making it impossible for anyone to stand on it.

This, and the cleanup that followed, has little to do with either this story or how we won the war, but it sticks in my mind, years later, when I ponder how the gods have treated me through the years.

I spent quite some time on this fast moving ship which, on its many, many missions with the ever increasing Pacific fleet, went nearly 230 thousand nautical miles - mostly in circles. It's all recorded in detail in a yearbook-type publication named "Flight Quarters" which is dedicated to the eighty men of the ship's company and the eighty-five fliers from her who "paid the supreme sacrifice," during the eleven war cruises. Much that it did has found its way into other history books.

(See: http://www.navsource.org/archives/02/24.htm and www.historycentral.com/Navy/cruiser/CV24 BellauWoods.html)

The Belleau Wood took the brunt of the first Kamikaze attack.

Four of its fliers went right through all the protective fire and dropped four torpedoes to sink a huge Japanese carrier; three pilots and crews eventually returned to the ship. Although this story is recorded in great detail in *Time* magazine of July 3, 1944, I've got to digress for a personal version. We couldn't mention it in letters home (because of censorship) until we read it in the Armed Forces Mini Edition of *Time*.

Here's how I wrote it to my wife (after we received the July 3 *Time*):

> Our planes went into an attack just as hazardous as the one they had seen Tojo try the day before - except that Tojo threw fifteen times as many planes into it. Not one of Tojo's had gotten through. Each of our four scored a perfect torpedo hit, and three of them - with their crews - are back aboard ship.
>
> It makes one think the Japs would see they are not even a second-rate outfit and would give up trying to play in the big time.
>
> Tate, one of my particularly good poker-playing buddies, held back the best part of the story. A bullet went right through his thumb when his control stick was shot away. The trigger for his forward guns was on top of the stick and was, of course, out of commission. His after-guns jammed while strafing the deck of the carrier as they went by. When he came up on

two Zekes (new name for Zeros), they were in perfect position to get him.

He pulled the biggest bluff of his life. He pointed the nose gun at one and, in so doing, had the tail guns pointed at the other. <u>They both left before they discovered that none of the guns could fire.</u> Brownie had let sinking a carrier become almost an obsession with him, and I'm sure he died happy.

Further detail would be much as you have read except that it just happened that the only pilot who tried to land on our little flight deck was an old college buddy I hadn't seen since 1939.

Most of them landed in the water.

The fleet's squadron had chased the Jap fleet at maximum range knowing they'd have to land in the water in the dark.

It, after overhaul from the Kamikaze, and with a completely green air squadron, made the first carrier strike on Tokyo. My "black gang" just kept the machinery going and got most of our "dope" from the smoke watch or from off duty trips to the flight deck.

Finally, as seniority worked its wonders, I became first assistant engineering officer - one day senior to a career Navy man who could really handle the job. I pointed out to the chief engineer that, under such conditions, the chief would never get relieved himself.

Here was a fact of life, which is as true today as it was then, and a flaw in every organization. There seems to be no answer. The better qualified is kept and the lesser is sent to some other station. In a case such as this - where everyone is trying to figure a way to get back to the States - this policy fostered a lot of mediocrity. It also created a lot of problems for those struggling to get new ships manned.

I think, particularly, of a foreign born machinist's mate who'd put in twenty years in the Navy without ever learning to read or write English. When the Bureau of Personnel issued orders to promote to chief anyone with 20 years in, he was immediately promoted and sent back to new construction.

All my children have thumbed through the book "Flight Quarters" (Copyright 1946 by John W. Alexander, Lieutenant, U S N R), and none have failed to note that all the pictures are of white men with one single exception. S-2 Division is all colored (Negro or Philippine) - except for the supply department officer to whom the colored were directly responsible. "They serve the Wardroom, the Warrant Officers Mess, the Captain's special pantry, and the officers' pantry, which is open 24 hours a day. They also clean the officers' rooms and take care of their laundry. At battle stations the nucleus is assigned to repair parties, to stand by as stretcher bearers and at battle dressing stations..." There are over fifty colored in the group picture - as compared to the seventy in my boiler division, which created all the power for the ship, its light, its water evaporation system, and its stability. The officers had the best of it in most ways.

Only once do I recall any comment or controversy over this situation. That's when the Marine Captain (from Virginia) came late from a hectic attack in rough seas (his gun, on the bow, was often under heavy seas and took longer to "secure" after attacks) and sat down to await his steak. He was told, "I'm sorry suh, they ain't no mo' — just enough fo' us boys." I remember, on the other hand, that after the wardroom had been used for hours as an emergency hospital; and after 97 of the 254 casualties from the Kamikaze were in sickbay and 72 awaiting burial, the wardroom was transformed into the beautiful dining room it always was. The clean napkins (which came weekly) were in place.

Recorded in the book "Flight Quarters" is the fact that the "boys" from S2 won most all honors at boxing, volleyball, and basketball. These were programs organized by the physical fitness officer who was known to everyone as the Tunneyfish. He was the product of a physical fitness program headed by Gene Tunney and manned, almost exclusively, by all-American athletes. Our physical fitness officer was 6'6", 235 pounds and amazingly agile.

If there is a message to come from all this re-hashing of a war that hits modern schoolboys (and most of their teachers) as distant history, it is the fact that, as I noted at the time, "It takes complete autocracy to preserve democracy." I've glossed over the highlights of my little part in each of three, distinctive kinds of Navy. I've never mentioned any dissension or protest - although it was perfectly legal for anyone to insist, through channels, on bringing anything to the attention of the Captain, the Admiral and on up to the Commander-in-Chief. Courts martial, theft, fights, drinking aboard ships, dereliction of duty - anything above and beyond the grousing and scuttlebutt which was necessary to relieve boredom - was practically unheard of. This was in spite of the fact that the mere haste of things made for multitudes of misfits and injustices.

Through the years there were thousands who worked under my direct orders. Only once did I put one on report. A young hillbilly said, "Nope, I ain't-a gonna do it," while we were at battle stations.

At his captain's mast he explained he got scared "locked up down there where I don't know what's-a goin' on."

After five days of bread and water in the brig, he was assigned to a deck division where he could be closer to the action. There, when the bosun's mate assigned him to lookout duty, he came up with the same answer, "Nope, I ain't-a gonna do it," and found himself locked into a little compartment - all alone with the anchor chain. After the Kamikaze hit, someone, checking the compartment for battle damage, let him out. Later that night, after all was calm, this same kid slipped by a sleeping (unheard of) Marine sentry into the Captain's cabin to shake him awake. To the startled skipper he said, "Captain, suh, I jus' wanted to know if the Admiral give ya hell for almost gittin' us sunk."

That earned him a trip to San Francisco and a medical discharge. Maybe that's what he was after all the time. It's hard to figure things like that.

Generally, though, everyone "followed the book" which, thank God, had been well written during peacetime when career people had time to figure things out. There'd have been hell to pay if there wasn't a plan, and immediate compliance, to go with Admiral Bull Halsey's order to "turn 180 degrees and increase to flank speed." What if he'd decided to take a vote!

There was, of course, a little foolishness to pass away the time.

Just after our strikes on Tokyo, a communications officer "let slip" to the barber that we were going back to San Francisco again - on June 31. He wanted to see how far and how fast the "straight dope" would travel before someone realized that there is no such thing as June 31.

It took quite awhile.

Instead we went to Iwo Jima to give air cover to those thousands of real heroes who took an awful beating in assaulting this fortress so near the Japanese homeland.

We steamed back and forth a couple of hundred miles off shore listening to the radio talk and following progress on maps in the wardroom - much like watching the world series.

Then, as we headed for Ulithi anchorage, the same fun loving communicator came to me with a message inviting commanding officers to transfer excess senior personnel to the rear for reassignment. Before he got around to telling me that it was directed to air group commanders, I had our engineering yeoman draw up my transfer papers and got down to the chief engineer with them for his approval.

———————

This is how I got into that other Navy - the one of McHale, and Queeg, and Mr. Roberts.

While in a launch, being transported across the harbor headed east, a Jap plane, from parts unknown, dropped a bomb in the vicinity of a ship about ten miles from the one we were approaching.

It was a strange feeling to see the elation of the crewmembers as we boarded. They, as civilians there, would get bonuses and combat pay as a result of this little visit. This didn't seem quite fair.

They carried several hundred "ambulatory wounded" Marines who had been evacuated from Iwo Jima.

As we approached Pearl Harbor, the Marine doctors were ordered to reexamine the patients and to transfer any who might be ready to reenter combat within thirty days at Pearl Harbor. Those who were more severely wounded were to go on to the United States.

The major told me that 100 percent insisted they would be ready in thirty days.

One of the doctors told me that he had never seen such an outbreak of "battle fatigue."

I guess it's the same today. Parris Island doesn't homogenize people either.

Anyway.

I ended up in a "pool" in Pearl Harbor, with orders to report to ComServPac (Commander Service Forces, Pacific), at 10 o'clock each morning.

During the greatly appreciated idle hours, I ran into my old friend Pete Bonan (who, while waiting for the Baltimore to get built in Boston, had sworn that someday he would come back and do something about those greatly overpriced and outmoded apartments in the West End ...).

We spent lots of time together with no responsibility but to report at ten each morning.

Finally came the day that I was told to report to a particular officer in the ComServPac building. He asked me: "What do you know about a reciprocating engine?"

My only answer was: "Nothing at all except that they exist."

He scribbled some notes and a couple of diagrams on some sheets of paper (that were intended to show me what was probably wrong with it). He handed these to me, along with my flight orders to New Caledonia and my assignment as chief engineering officer of the USS Naos - a liberty ship that had been converted to a troop-carrying transport.

(See:http://www.navsource.org/archives/09/130105.htm)

Aboard the plane I was seated next to a much older man whose orders called for him to take over as Commanding Officer of the same ship. We were, of course, curious as to why both vacancies would exist simultaneously.

When we arrived at this little French colony in the South Pacific we discovered that the ship was not there. An available lieutenant and the warrant machinist had been temporarily assigned to take her to New Zealand.

There was a nice little resort-type hotel that was the headquarters for transient officers, as well as for a group of New Zealand Red Cross workers. There was a dance scheduled for the first night we arrived and the skipper, somewhat in jest, dared me to get him a date for the dance. There were, perhaps, thirty feminine Red Cross workers and, including the operational staff and the ships afloat, probably 2,000 U.S. Navy officers in this little town. I inquired around and, much to the surprise of both of us, arranged a blind date for the skipper-to-be.

When I asked him, next morning, how things had worked out he said, "Well, I'll tell you. I don't know what might have happened had I tried, but just at a quick look, if she opened her mouth, her teeth would have fallen out and, if she'd taken off her dress, her bones would have fallen apart."

While lounging about the bar in this nice little hotel, we noted all the hundreds of peculiar little marks on the ceiling. We were told they came when the place ran out of every kind of drink but champagne, and the clients had contests to see who could hit the ceiling with the popping cork.

Now we must digress a little into things I didn't personally see or participate in so you will get the proper picture of what we'd walked in to.

We were still curious as to how a ship could need us both at once and what her "track record" had been.

She had, before we arrived, carried upwards of 17,000 passengers, "ranging from beauteous USO Field Units to fighting Marines, salty sailors, versatile Seabees, slogging soldiers, cocky New Zealand troops, star-studded aviators, and a company of the famed Fijian Scouts." The general cargo in her spacious holds had varied from huge "General Sherman tanks to genuine Japanese souvenirs (custom built by ingenious Seabees)." Most of the cargo, however, had consisted of rolling stock, aviation spare parts and the multitudinous necessities for maintaining advance bases.

All this activity, ordered by the port director at Noumea, had kept her hopping the islands of the South Pacific, without a proper rest, for seventeen months.

Just prior to our arrival she had taken a group of Seabees to Pago Pago in American Samoa.

There the skipper and the chief engineer had had "their" Jeep (which had been acquired somewhere along the way but wasn't standard equipment) set ashore, and they disappeared for several days in some distant native village. When it came time for the ship to shove off, they were still among the missing

The governor had come down to the dock - with a band - to see her off.

About the time the band had run out of repertory, the Jeep, loaded with native girls and two "loaded Gentlemen," came to a skidding stop at the gangway.

The skipper, as soon as he reached the bridge, thumbed his nose at the impatient governor and called for full speed astern - while drowning out the exhausted band with the whistle.

The propeller had become entangled with the anchor line of a buoy, and the damage done to the stern tube bearings was to stay with this ship until her demise.

As soon as practicable, the ship's doctor ordered that the skipper, the chief engineer, and the boatswain (who was drinking hair tonic) be sent home as chronic alcoholics. This had created our two positions - and one promotion.

At the doctor's insistence that the whole crew was "going Asiatic," the port director in Noumea had "arranged" a trip to New Zealand by rounding up all the trucks and jeeps on the island that needed repairs and sending them to Auckland. While the repairs were made, the crew played. Key officers for this relatively simple trip were assigned from the transients available in the hotel.

In due time the ship returned - with the repaired vehicles and the relaxed crew - and edged up to her berth.

The prescribed change of command ceremony was as brief as possible and, in accordance with regulations, each new officer first looked into his roomsafe to check it out.

I was amazed to discover that my safe was loaded "to the gills" with an assortment of New Zealand scotch, rye, and brandy. At that moment my telephone rang. It was the skipper - who hadn't been able to wait any longer to show me that his was the same. "I want you, as soon as you leave, to get hold of the executive officer and tell him that there'll be no more drinking aboard this ship - with the port holes open." At that he lowered the black painted port hole cover and poured me the first drink I'd ever had aboard a Navy ship (except a brandy or two, which had been contributed by a teetotaling pilot each of whom received one from the doctor after almost every air battle).

Then we discussed our first impression of this "old rust bucket."

Ethnics slipped in for the first time in years. The skipper had been a yacht skipper for the DuPonts in Miami, and the executive officer was a Jewish lawyer from Chicago. The skipper had already decided they could never get along. The cargo officer was a professional seaman from the Merchant Marine and "certainly should have the exec's job but couldn't be replaced as a cargo handler." The supply officer was a "college boy" from Yale. The doctor had done his seven-year stint in surgery in a Catholic hospital just before the Navy grabbed him. (We soon learned it was he who had stocked our safes.)

We were the only two among the fifteen officers and 150 men who had been in any sort of combat. Our orders were to head into what had been highly defended Jap positions but were now pretty well neutralized - except for the last one. We were to make stops at Guadalcanal, Russell Islands, Enewitok, and Ulithi, before delivering our Seabee unit to Okinawa - which was still under daily Kamikaze attack and generally protected from these flights by a heavy smoke screen. It was obvious that the crew must be "shaped up," so discipline, drill, and target practice became the order of the day, most every day.

I studied out my engine - the like of which I had never seen. It was referred to either as "a knee-action turbine" or "a clanking monster." It had been built in an iron works in Sunnyvale, California and had never had more than the most rudimentary maintenance. Sure enough, one of the 16" Bobbitt bearings needed adjustment, just as the man at Pearl Harbor had told me. We fixed this. The main steam line had leaked since the day of commissioning but there had never been an opportunity to let the pressure off and approach the leak to find out why. (We finally, after "mothballing," discovered that a bolt had been omitted from the flanged joint when the ship was built).

An intricate little "gadget" that could check the valve settings for peak efficiency was still sealed, in its original box, and stored in the closet of my cabin. I read the directions, tried it on, made some adjustments, and got a couple more turns (per minute) out of the old bucket. This, however, made the propeller shaft whip a little more near the damaged stern tube bearing - which was constantly "lubricated" with salt water leaking in and which we constantly pumped out.

There wasn't much else to do. It was like an old steam locomotive; it would run forever if given enough steam and oil. We couldn't do anything about the boilers.

This gave me lots of time to talk with "the doc" who was, by all odds, the most interesting character I'd ever met.

He was the acme of frustration.

The only legitimate problem he had encountered was - on the first day out, about a year and a half before - when a bulldozer blade dropped down the back of a passenger lounging near it.

He had, since then, done all the tonsillectomies, appendectomies, circumcisions, etc. he could scrape up among passengers and crew alike.

He'd married just before leaving the States, made twins, gotten leave to go see them, and now had "three kids, after only three days of married life at home."

In accordance with regulations, he advised me every time he was going to perform surgery - so I could make certain that the water and/or electrical supply didn't give him any problems.

One day I asked him who he'd operated on the night before. He casually replied, "Myself." He opened up his fly to show me the sutures in his testicles where he had sterilized himself. I was, of course, no less than aghast as he explained it really was very simple.

"I just had to psyche myself up for it by telling my hands that they were here and that the patient was down there."

Then he continued, "Why don't you come watch tonight - I'm going to do it to the skipper" (who was over fifty).

I did go back to his well-equipped "sickbay" and noted what a simple procedure it was with his well-trained medic by his side. When I later asked him why he hadn't waited for his own operation until we were in some port with a hospital, he said, "They'd all know I'm a Catholic from my training, and we're opposed to such operations as this - whether we have three kids in three days or not."

————————

The ship's supply officer had, during the trip to New Zealand, picked up a lot of "lamb" and a batch of sheepskin coats - which we all felt certain had come from the same critters.

The doc had always picked his own menu, to maintain his fine physique. As others of us started to put in special orders, on the night that lamb was served, the supply officer instructed the mess attendants that there would be no more special menus for anyone.

When the night came that the doc, sitting right next to the "kid from Yale," was served a salad when the menu called for lamb, the kid (young Bursie) excused himself and headed for the pantry where he could be heard "blasting" the mess attendant who'd dared to disobey his orders.

As Bursie returned to his seat, the doc caught him with an uppercut that seemed to come right from the deck.

Bursie went shouting for the skipper.

"Looks to me like you ought to see the doctor first," said the skipper.

"He's the one who did it," squalled Bursie.

I was appointed as the one-man court martial. I also was instructed to sit down with the exec (a trained attorney) and figure a way to drop the charges that the supply officer made against the black mess attendant for insubordination.

We worked it out.

We also got "Bursie" to save the rest of the "lamb" for the passengers.

During this long and tiresome trek we held weekly Captain's Inspections - as required by the book.

The skipper had never liked the steam that hissed from the leaking main steam line right near the entrance to my little world and had always found some reason to skip the engine room on his weekly trips. This had created a problem in keeping my crew "on the ball" in the way of the old "spit and polish" Navy. It had become like "why clean the house if no one's coming to visit."

So, I finally talked him into descending the fifty or so feet down to the bilge plates where my clanking monster manufactured heat, the smell of overheated oil, and the power (12,500 HP) needed to propel this 450' long "bucket of bolts."

I'd forewarned my crew that the skipper really was coming today, and everything looked beautiful. It took him about thirty seconds to decide this and head for the exit.

When we hit fresh air again, he turned to me and said, "You know, you don't raise enough hell."

"Why?"

"Because the men didn't snap to attention the way they should have."

We "laid over" three weeks at Eniwetok and two weeks at Ulithi, while the fiercest battle of the war was still raging at Okinawa.

My old alma mater, the COLORADO, with her 31,500 tons of firepower and armor plate, had been one of 1213 ships that had spent many previous weeks assaulting this bastion, 700 miles beyond the Japanese home islands. They had been attacked by everything that was left of the Jap navy, including hundreds of Kamikaze planes.

Soldiers and marines had finally stormed ashore and found old men and little children to be their fiercest surviving enemies.

Eventually it was considered safe for us to enter the now crowded Buckner Bay and try to arrange for facilities with which to unload our assorted construction cargo. There were still occasional suicide planes and an almost constant smoke screen.

I will long remember one choice bit of repartee I picked up while watching the stevedores. An officer yelled down to some big black Seabee stevedore, "Can't you see what'll happen if you rig it that way?"

Right back came, "Boss, if I could see what'd happen all the time, I'd be the boss."

We took advantage of this opportunity to try to readjust the main bearings on our clanking monster to take some of the slap out of them. We had them all dismantled when emergency orders came to get under way immediately. As we hurriedly put them back together, it was inevitable that accuracy was sacrificed.

The emergency was a typhoon warning, and our orders were to be the first, of three hundred ships in the anchorage, to leave through the single narrow inlet.

Yes, you guessed it.

Just at the crucial point, one of the big bronze eight-inch bearings began to "seize." Oil poured on to it simply went up in smoke. I called the skipper to tell him we must stop immediately.

"Can't stop - we'll block the outlet" was all he could say.

I looked around at old Chief Harger (chief machinist's mate with near twenty years in the China Station Navy, who was on this ship because he was too big for the manholes in combat ships). He was whittling old brown soap into his laundry bucket and seemed totally unconcerned.

In a few moments he got a broom and started sloshing the heavy suds onto the now screeching bearing. It calmed down and so did we. We went on a few hundred yards, dropped the hook, loosened up the bearing, got underway again, and regained our position as lead ship of the convoy.

When I got time, later that day, I searched the manual of engineering instructions. Sure enough, right there in black and white, long before the war, the men of the old Navy had written this exact procedure for dealing with such an emergency.

The typhoon, which we were skirting, was one of the worst ever. We were without cargo or ballast and the screw constantly jumped out of the water - causing the engine to race. We kept a man at the emergency cut-off throttle to try to catch the rhythm and avoid this as much as possible.

The waves were so tremendous that even a ship of this size would capsize unless steered directly into the wind. Six ships, that lost steering control, were never heard from again.

(See: http://www.history.navy.mil/faqs/faq102-6.htm)

When, three days later, we returned to Buckner Bay, the havoc we saw was unbelievable. Small craft, landing barges, and one big ship loaded with ammunition littered the beaches. The ammunition ship had, presumably because of the volatility of its cargo, been ordered to ride out the storm in the nearly empty harbor. It had, with both anchors down and engines set at full speed ahead, been blown back several miles across the immense Buckner Bay, to end up stern to, on the other side of this bay that accommodated 300 ships at moorings.

The post office had blown away, as had all the signal towers, and the majority of the buildings.

Our hasty departure had left Lt. Bursie and an assistant on the beach looking for some way to get rid of the fifty-three million dollars' worth of invasion currency that had been entrusted to him for delivery to Korea.

To retrace our steps a little is the only way to explain this problem.

While we were waiting in Ulithi, the skipper suggested I get together with the exec (so we could make full use of his legal background) and write a real blockbuster to the Bureau of Ships concerning all the mechanical problems of our old worn-out tub – so we could get ordered home to San Francisco. The facts had been properly presented and the orders had come. We were to pick up some B-29 pilots and crews, deliver our money cargo, and return to San Francisco via Pearl Harbor.

Now back to the money. "Bursie" had discovered someone willing to sign for his cargo and take it off our hands so that we could avoid the extra trip. He, and the enlisted man he had taken ashore with him, got left behind when we ran from the typhoon. They had thrown the meat out of a portable refrigerator and ridden out the storm in it.

When the storm was over we proceeded with his plan of "toting" the precious cargo overland around the harbor to the other ship - guarded by a platoon of Marines.

Some unimaginative bureaucrat had been "foresighted" enough to disguise the cargo. He had marked it as Scotch Whiskey. Of course, the inevitable happened. One case was missing when it arrived at its destination.

A retracing of the route found a million dollars worth of Jap currency blowing around in the defoliated jungle and an explanation that it must have fallen off the truck.

I would presume that, had it been labeled Japanese currency, the shipment would have arrived intact.

We had an uneventful trip back with the engine being carefully nursed and everyone dreaming of stateside liberty.

As we neared Pearl Harbor, a target drone was flown by for target practice, and our little guns started peppering away at it.

Suddenly a shell exploded in the face of a young seaman.

The Doc had his second legitimate customer in nearly two years of war.

He easily saved one of the kid's eyes, then went doggedly to work on the other - picking minute pieces of powder and brass out of it, to the total of some fifty - and saved it, too.

It was while he was still operating that we heard the Japs had surrendered.

On our arrival in Pearl, we were immediately boarded by an inspection team who decided we could make one more trip after a short availability in the yard cleared up the worst of our problems.

We were also ordered to put ashore any excess personnel.

Somewhere in the South Pacific we had acquired a refrigeration machinist mate, along with the five huge Army refrigerators that had been tied down to our main deck and plugged in with extension cords. They had, of course, been necessary when additional holds were converted to troop carrying space. We had no spare parts for them and couldn't find any in any Navy yard.

When I finally got to the commodore with this problem, his words were quick, "Were you ordered to transfer this man?"

"Yes, Sir."

"Transfer him."

Our "cargo" for this one last trip was seven hundred and eighty-six Okinawan prisoners of war, a group of some fifty Army guards (who had been among the troops who had captured them) and all the food we could cram into limited storage spaces - knowing that there would be none available at the other end of the trip because of the typhoon.

While all this was taking place there were some interesting bull sessions and goings on at the Officers' Club and, I'm sure, even more heated ones wherever enlisted men gathered.

A group of us, bemoaning our situation in general, were gathered around the doc drinking French 75s (half brandy half champagne) when Doc came up with the bright idea, "If I told someone I sterilized myself they'd send me home as psycho."

Just then a doctor I'd known on another ship walked by and I put the hypothetical question to him.

"Why, the son-of-a-bitch would be crazy," was his immediate retort.

At another time I ran across the Boston Wool Merchant who had been my wife's boss in Maine. He'd counted up enough "points" to allow him to request immediate release. That morning, he'd received word that his long-sought divorce from an alcoholic wife had become final. He was, therefore, no longer eligible for release. He, too, was drinking French 75s.

Before long we were on our way - about twenty days straight to Okinawa. After several of the days had gone by it came to the attention of the Army major, in charge of the prisoners, that one of them had set up shop in a small compartment deep in the bowels of the ship and was "taking care" of the sex urges, which were pretty strong in most of our crew. The major set up a watch and caught our best quartermaster. He made a formal report to the skipper and insisted on a court-martial on the grounds that our crew was mingling with his prisoners.

The skipper (who still never talked directly to the executive officer) told me to form the court-martial and to get the exec to show me how to let this kid off with a clean record while still placating the major.

The first step was to find interpreters. The major provided us with a list of three, whom we proceeded to interview.

The first was an old man who had been a Peruvian schoolteacher and could speak Peruvian but not English. None of our crew spoke Peruvian.

The second was a wise looking little apple who said, "I talk good English" but, when pressed further, could say nothing else. Some GI in the interrogation camp had taught him to say those four words when he got to the head of the line.

The third was a twelve-year-old kid (who we were assured had been captured with a rifle in his hands) who could speak English very well.

After a short conference the exec suggested that we rule that the testimony that would come out in this trial should not be heard by one so young.

We, therefore, decided that there could be no trial because there was no way to communicate.

After that, the compartment was securely locked.

———————

In line with the theme of this little tale - which is that people don't easily homogenize - I should quote, verbatim, a letter I sent to my wife on Sept. 18, 1945.

My Darling -

We had a funeral this morning - about the least spectacular ever, I guess. When our prisoners came aboard, one could barely climb the gangway, even with a buddy carrying his sea bag. The Doc had checked him over when he came on board and said he would die soon - no matter what anyone did. He had been laying out on deck without eating ever since. About three this morning he started breathing real hard. The guard called a couple of his countrymen and the doctor. By four he was dead. At 5:30 the engine room called to tell me we had just stopped. I got up to see why and found that the dead prisoner had been sewed up in a canvas sack, with a couple of five inch shells for weights, and had been dumped over the bow - right where he died. The engine was stopped for a couple of minutes to be sure he didn't get caught in the screw. Customarily the dead are carried to the stern and dumped without stopping the engine, but I guess it was easier this way. He was a civilian Okinawan, about 45 years old, with some unfamiliar kind of stomach worms eating on him.

The guards are all soldiers who were injured at Okinawa and have since been hospitalized and released and are now returning to their units there. A sergeant was telling me that the little fellows I mentioned, who didn't look so mean, were the worst sort of enemy - that one ran into his foxhole with a hand grenade and laid down with four American soldiers in the hole until it went off. The sergeant says he happened to live through it.

An Army captain was going to read a Protestant church service this morning for the funeral but an Okinawan volunteered to hold the service instead. He didn't do or say anything - just signaled for the men to dump his countryman.

Men were sleeping all over the deck while the boatswain's mate was sewing up the corpse - they didn't even wake up. The volunteer preacher had to step over a sleeping man to get near enough to the body to signal for them to dump him over with no ceremony.

Soon after it was over reveille sounded and the men got up, wiped their eyes, and formed in line for chow.

Don't know why I write this except as another possible insight into the peculiar oriental mind - death just didn't seem to mean a thing. Maybe they were sort of envious of him."

These people were not troops, as such. They were real dregs - the Home Guard, who had been poorly organized and equipped for the purpose of a last ditch defense.

The United States - with wars in the Pacific and in Europe - had uniformed slightly over 10 per cent of its population. The rest were considered either too old, too young, physically unfit, or needed for some civilian use in the creation of the multitude of war materials that would be wasted away.

This totally uncalled-for war was the colossal result of the failure to create a proper peace after the war that had preceded it by a generation. The failure to properly sew up the wounds of this latest one has created continuing war, and near war, through the next two generations.

Still, we continue to get weaker and weaker while our enemies get stronger and stronger - just as though we hadn't learned a thing. The Japs were beaten at Midway, but they knew we were too, so they fought for three more years.

After debarking the troops and starting to unload cargo (onto lighters in the middle of Buckner Bay), we had an almost exact rerun of the previous typhoon.

Our engine and its boilers had suffered severely from the slipshod work that had been accomplished in the too-short time allowed at Pearl Harbor. We sent, as we stopped in Eniwetok, an even more urgent letter to BuShips stating that we must be deactivated.

This time I was really worried that we would not survive the wild seas of the typhoon, but the gods were with us.

When we got back to Buckner Bay there was even worse havoc than before, aggravated by the fact that everywhere there were groups of people: Army,

Navy, and Marines, who had certified orders to catch the "first available" transportation to San Francisco or any other West Coast port. This was the beginning of the much-heralded "magic carpet" that would start heroes back to whatever future awaited them in civilian life.

We emptied our holds of everything but enough food for a thousand men for a month and started taking on passengers. Most of them were astray from their units, had lost all their gear, and had been sleeping in caves and mud holes through the storm.

We got clearance from the port captain for a new route across the ocean. The "great circle," which was the shortest route, would have taken us, after a couple of days, within a 100 miles of Japan, and all along the Aleutians.

The skipper figured, in view of the shortage of foul weather gear, blankets, and proper heat for the holds, a more Southern route was much preferred.

We steamed due east for 800 miles, then started the "great circle."

This never before used sea-lane led us to twenty-five days of uninterrupted monotony. Not a ship, not an airplane, not an island, practically not even a bird, ever came into view as we nursed this worn out old bucket full of war-weary troops (most of whom had imagined a finer "magic carpet") toward the Golden Gate.

During this long trip there was one little problem I was called on to get into because the skipper still didn't like direct contact with the exec and didn't feel well grounded in legal matters himself.

One of our motley and over capacity batch of passengers had decided to become an entrepreneur. He'd written a vivid account of his stay in Okinawa. It involved the deaths of fifty U. S. servicemen who'd taken refuge in a cave. Unbeknownst to them it had been used, either by the Japs or our own army or marines, as an ammunition cache. They'd lit a fire and been blown to bits.

It was a well-written little pamphlet and was selling like the proverbial hot cakes, at 50 cents per copy, when the skipper got wind of it. Some sort of intuition told him that it wouldn't look good in the newspapers - particularly in view of the fact it happened after the Japs had capitulated. Some other part of his thinking apparatus brought up the constitution and freedom of the press.

When the exec and I finished discussing the matter, it was decided if the publisher were to repurchase each and every copy (and prove to our satisfaction they'd all been returned), we would not prosecute him.

For what?

For misappropriation of government property by way of the paper, ink and mimeograph stencils that had been used.

I never heard any more of that story so we must have gotten all of them.

The order of each day was to get in the chow line, get your ration, and get a spot back in line for the next meal.

As we neared the Golden Gate, a USO ship - complete with voluptuous volunteers and a band - came out to greet us and steam alongside us to the pier.

Of course, long before we got there the inevitable line had formed at the gangway and the minute it was in place, the Exodus commenced.

The port captain (obviously the relief for an experienced one who had amassed enough "points" to go home) fought his way up through the crowd to explain to our skipper that the moment our passengers disembarked we must clear the dock, for the ship behind us, and go out to anchor in the middle of San Francisco Harbor to await further orders. At the question about liberty for our crew, he quickly withdrew.

This word spread like wildfire throughout the ship so we immediately stationed a couple of master-at-arms at the gangway to make certain none of our crew got mixed in with the passengers. At least ninety percent of the 150-man crew and thirteen of the fifteen officers had been away from the States for a solid two years. And now, after this tremendous welcome home, they couldn't even get to a telephone.

After we were anchored and the engine had been "secured," the skipper called me to his cabin. No further orders had come. I should tell the executive officer to await them while we went ashore in the skipper's little whaleboat (which a bunch of eager seabees had fancied up into a Captain's Gig). We would, somehow, dig up some liberty boats for our crew.

Three hours later we had exhausted every possibility, sent back a message that there would be no liberty, and settled down to French 75s. It was a shock to find the difference in price. We weren't in the mood, anyway, and after each of us had called his wife, we headed back to the ship to study the bustling harbor from afar with the rest of those to whom we had grown so close.

The next day, when liberty boats were finally rounded up there were an almost unbelievable number of reasons why everyone had to go ashore, so we cut those kept aboard far below the "skeleton crew" level.

Chief Harger, the 300-pounder who'd saved our bacon during the typhoon, waited until everyone else had been ashore at least twice. Then he went for three days and came back in such condition that he was brought aboard in a cargo net.

In due time we got orders to prepare to decommission by following the routine established for "mothballing" a ship. This meant thoroughly cleaning and covering with preservative every piece of machinery "not essential" for the last trip up the river to the ever-growing nest of mothballed ships. This meant little to us because we needed everything but one boiler to move.

All food, ship's store supplies, tools, etc., were to be "given" to the nearest naval activity. This was generally taken to mean the one who got there first. Good old Harger made me up a big wooden box full of home maintenance tools and toiletries and shipped them to my wife's address by Navy freight - at no cost, of course.

Title B Items were different. They included guns, ammunition, delicate instruments, furniture, cooking and dining utensils, refrigerators and other such things that might have a salvage value. They were all the responsibility of the Supply Officer and were to be disposed of by him. He came to the skipper with the problem that he could find no one to take the five big, room-size, army refrigerators off the main deck.

A simple solution.

With no orders from anywhere, we simply lifted anchor, pulled in at a dock beside a big traveling crane, and signaled to the operator to lift them off and set them on the dock. Bursie had him sign for them and that problem was solved. We pulled out, went back to our anchorage and proceeded to moth-ball.

Down in the engine room there was Harger's pride and joy, which had been helpful through most of the two years in keeping his weight up. He had created, from a smashed water bubbler, a couple of tool boxes, some fiberglass insulation and other mis-cellaneous parts, a refrigerator that was for the ex-clusive use of the "black gang" - and was carefully secreted in preparation for each Captain's inspec-tion. He now found need for it in his apartment since home appliances were in mighty short supply in the stores. It belonged to no one and I told him to take it. He was back shortly with the request that I give a written chit that it was his personal property - otherwise the Marine at the gate wouldn't let him out with it. The easier solution came quickly to mind, and I told him to meet me outside the gate. I got in the same Jeep with the same box beside me, drove to the same Marine at the same gate, and was greeted simply with a crisp salute. Harger took over and I walked back in.

Weeks ran into months, releases from active duty kept coming, our crew kept shrinking.

The skipper, the doc, the exec, and practically everyone else was gone when Whitten, the ex-cargo officer now turned skipper, finally got word for us to take the old bucket up the river to the "bone yard." We were followed by a motor launch that would bring the final eight of us back to civilian life. We nudged her in alongside a twin and went through the ship, as prescribed, with the keeper of the yard so that Bursie could get his receipt and we could be off. When the keeper heard the water gurgling in through the stern tube he threw up his hands. There was "no way" that he could accept it. He had no provisions for pumping it out.

I remembered the last jug of New Zealand brandy, still in my safe, and suggested we "sit down and reason together."

After about an hour of discussing our mutual problems, the jug was empty, and the receipt signed. We scrambled down the ladder to our launch and headed for the separation center.

———

I've gone into a lot of detail that shows this pre-planned, diversionary war - which had no apparent basis in ideology or enmity - through my eyes. Very few got the same picture. Historians have taken mountains of material and condensed it into less space. I have omitted tremendous amounts of material, they never saw, in the interest of brevity. I realize that the ninety- percent who didn't wear gold braid got quite a different picture. I realize that those pilots who survived it, and their crews, were a completely different breed - who got a completely different picture during their much briefer tours of duty.

The "airdales," who would scoot across the deck to throw stray-armed rockets overboard, were a clear different breed from Chief Harger. It takes all kinds to make a Navy - let alone an Army, a Marine Corps, or a Coast Guard. Think how much more to make a United States civilian population, a free world, or a world.

The point, though, is that despite the hasty training and expansion, both in the services themselves and in the fabulous war machine that supplied them, there was a sense of unity and cooperation. It wasn't flawless, but it outshone the polarity of the modern nation.

I won't dwell on this because it's so apparent and so changeable day by day.

Certainly, though, the leaders of the forties wouldn't be simultaneously watching the disintegration of American interest in four key waterways and the key fuel supply nor would the people of that day have sat apathetically by and allowed it to happen.

Now let's go back to the start and see if we can't find out why Gramps should know more about these things than even your teacher, maybe.

"When I was a boy" should mean more than just an excuse to close up the mind because the old fogey is all mixed up and doesn't know what he's talking about.

The Gramps who is writing this was born in 1916. Anyone who was ten years younger or twenty years older was, somehow or other, involved in the second war to end all wars - and has his own personal stories of the times, which are well worth listening to. Mine are just about average. Many went back to Korea where they were ordered to fight with their hands tied. Some even went to Vietnam where, worse than being tied, they were spat upon.

The "thing," now, is to believe that wars are created for the purpose of justifying the existence of the Pentagon and enhancing the profits of the munitions makers - defense is no longer a proper adjective.

The idea of liberty is a bygone concept because, in an effort to force it on everyone - whether they want it or not, the lawmakers have snatched it away from those who did want it. Along with it, they have snatched the incentives that created it.

Origins

Anyway.

Here goes.

When I was a boy I had five older and two younger brothers and sisters. My father, from my earliest memory, was in constant pain and much deformed in the hands and feet from rheumatoid arthritis. My mother had been a schoolteacher in Indiana.

Father was editor and publisher of a little weekly newspaper in Idaho Springs, Colorado, which was, I believe, the eighth newspaper he'd owned.

It had proven physically impossible for him to make a living for his growing family by the week-to-week operation of a paper but he had found that, if he could buy an ailing one cheap he could, then, iron out the wrinkles and resell it at a profit.

The price of gold had collapsed, and the returning GIs from WW1 had chosen to seek other opportunities than mining, so this paper had become practically worthless.

At my first memory we were still living upstairs over the closed-down newspaper plant. On weekends my father was commuting from Denver by way of the old Colorado and Southern narrow gauge line, which twisted its way up the canyon over a single pair of rails. It stopped at the station and proceeded another fourteen miles up to Georgetown, where it turned around on the famous "Georgetown Loop" and made its way back on the exact same rails.

The line had originally been built to carry ore and was, even then, a loser headed for extinction.

Father's job in Denver (the only one he ever had) was working for his younger brother - at wages just below subsistence.

The family quarters, where I was born, was, in every sense of the word, a cold water flat. The entire heating system was a big coal-burning kitchen range with a built-in reservoir next to the oven. This was the hot water supply. The bathtub was the wash tub.

On Saturday nights it was ceremoniously filled with dippers of water, both hot and cold and pulled out to the middle of the kitchen floor.

There, my twelve-year older sister would take her bath first and then assist in polishing up the rest of us.

Before my five-year-younger brother was born, Dad had, somehow, arranged to sell this old building and buy a suitable house a mile from the center of the town. It had a big fenced yard and a large barn.

He'd also sent big sister off to college and bought, from his brother, a 1920 Buick touring car, which he used for commuting.

Older brother Wayne soon joined the Navy and our next older brother, Earl, who was severely crippled with rheumatoid arthritis - so that he couldn't manage the walk to school - stayed in Denver with his grandmother.

There were lots of chores for the rest of us but lots of fun, too. Mother was quite an organizer, and we each knew when it was our turn to chop the wood, bring in the coal, empty the ashes, mow the lawn, churn the butter, trim around the fence, pump the washer, turn the wringer, etc.

What was fun then would be outrageous vandalism now, especially when we had a baby sitter.

Our house was on Miner (the main) Street, and every Sunday a constant parade of big White (painted red) sightseeing buses from Denver, passed our door. They were on their way up under the Georgetown Loop over Berthoud Pass, along the Trail Ridge of the Continental Divide, back via Estes Park to the Stanley Hotel (built by the inventor of the Stanley Steamer - which had been invented for the purpose of getting customers to the hotel).

Mixed in with these buses, were touring cars. (Now the Interstate to Vail goes through the back yard and has replaced the block behind.)

Early in the morning, before the action started, we would place a pocketbook - usually with a corner of a ten-dollar bill sticking out of it - out in the gravel street (which had just been wet down by the sprinkler truck as a method of dust control). We would carefully cover the string that led from the pocket-book up through our yard to the porch, where we gathered to watch the pocketbook trick work its magic.

When the first car stopped to pick it up (only to see it vanish), a long line of buses behind him would have to grind to a halt.

As soon as there was a break in the traffic we would get ready for the next one.

The Town Constable took a dim view of our simple pranks.

This didn't come, though, until we had gotten sort of tired of the pocketbook trick and decided it was more fun to roll old tires down the inside stairs, out the front door, down the sidewalk through the open gate and out into the traffic.

Anyway.

We decided to get even with this old fogey constable who had such a poor sense of humor.

On Halloween night, when we sort of had carte blanche, we picked up a privy and moved it about ten feet. Then we leaned a board up against the front door of the home of a little old lady who didn't appreciate us either. We put a big rock on the bottom of it and a couple of baskets full of leaves delicately balanced on top. Then we rang her doorbell.

Of course she called the constable to report that those Grass Valley brats had littered her hall with leaves.

Of course we stayed near the streetlight just long enough for the fuzz to spot us and then ran into the darkness - to hide behind the two-holer we'd moved.

Surely you've guessed by now that Butch had to go home and take a bath before he could protect any more citizens from the harmless pranks of the kids.

Fortunately, we soon moved to Denver.

I've included this just to point out that there's a little bit o' the divil in all o' us, and nobody's really a lost cause because he misbehaves in his youth.

———————

While we were in Grass Valley, where I walked the mile to school for the first three years (Mother had taught me so well at home that I started in the second grade), my mother did everything imaginable to help Dad hang onto the place. She baked tremendous batches of bread, rolls, coffeecake, etc. on the old coal stove and had us peddle them to people. She made beautiful floral arrangements from the big garden and turned them into cash. She fed us on mush and fried mush along with the vegetables from the garden. We bought chickens for killing and plucking from the widow woman down the street where we got our milk and eggs.

Still, in the middle of the Roaring Twenties - when everything was on the boom - we had to relinquish the house to the mortgage holder and move into a much too small flat next to Dad's brother's print shop on Welton Street in Denver.

The school I went to was, then even more than now, in the middle of the slums. Every race and color was in attendance. It was a total mystery to me. I had gotten straight A's in the mountain school. Here my first report card of the fifth grade was straight F's.

My four-year-older brother, Irvin, had found Manual Training High (the only high school available to a resident of this neighborhood) so dumbfounding that he'd quit and gone to work in a bakery long before the first grades came out.

It wasn't long until, to everyone's delight, our crippled-up father announced he'd bought another newspaper, The Longmont Ledger, about thirty miles due north of Denver. Father, Mother and the older brothers worked on it in one capacity or another while Mother kept house besides.

We lived in a nice house in a good neighborhood, for $40 a month, but found it a little crowded. Soon we moved to a bigger, older one, for $35.

I was too young to be much help at first so I got some cards printed and scoured the neighborhood for lawns to mow and driveways to shovel.

Irvin Guy Stafford in front of Longmont Ledger
(Elsie Mae Sheridan Stafford in window)

Brother Irvin was the sports writer and soon became Manager of the high school football team - proud possessor of a banner that was strung across Main Street before every big game - "Football Champions of America, 1908."

We still weren't too busy for a little devilment.

It wasn't long after we arrived that I got the bright idea of walking down Main Street in front of the theater and unscrewing the valve stems from the cars, which were angle-parked, each with one wheel up to the sidewalk. I thought Halloween was the same here as it had been in the mountains.

When I suddenly found myself in the "tank" of the jailhouse with all the town drunks, it may very well have been the best thing that ever happened to me. Only a couple of hours went by before the local police called my mother and had her come down to get me. It was, though, long enough to teach me to think of the possible consequences when, in the future, I would dream up another such stunt.

Soon I was in the Boy Scouts and really went for the program.

At 13 I was editor and publisher of The Boy Scout Booster, which was chartered by National Headquarters. I sold ads in it, and sold subscriptions to all the troops in the council. At 15, I was the youngest Eagle Scout in the Northern Colorado and Wyoming area and was instructor in cooking, model airplane making, and leather working at the area camp all summer.

Also, at 15, I had a responsible job at the Ledger Office.

Boy Scout Norman Sheridan Stafford

I would walk down the alley at 6 a.m. and light the gas burner for the Linograph machine. This consisted of filling the tank with gasoline, pumping up the air tank, which forced it to vaporize, filling a little pocket with alcohol (to preheat the burner under the lead pot), then lighting it off. Afterwards, I would sweep out the entire plant, stopping at each heating stove to fire it up.

After school I would sit with my Dad and "hold copy" as he read proof aloud. This was so we might find misspelled names, sentences that had been overlooked by the operator, etc. (This was a job, I presume, that didn't exist where the pay was much or the typesetter was competent.)

On publication day I would carry my route and then come back in time to finish with the mailing.

On Saturday I would gather all the slugs from the typesetting machine that had been used during the week, and all the trimmings that had gathered around it, to the back room to melt it down and "pig" it. This was done in a big coal-fired vat with a bellows. When the type metal was all melted, I would pour in the "flux" which would make a big cloud of smoke while bringing all the impurities to the top to be skimmed off. Then I would ladle the metal into ingot forms and, when cool, carry them back to the composing machine for reuse. I write this 45 years later simply to point out that this sort of exposure to lead - along with the many burns I got through the years from "squirts" of one kind or another - makes the lead paint rules of today look ridiculous - designed simply to help fuel the fires of inflation.

Father saw fit to pay me $2.50 per week for these services, probably on the theory that if I had this time available, I'd hustle that much somewhere else.

He finally, as so many times before, had so changed the image of this old rundown newspaper that he felt safe in looking for a profitable sale - in spite of the deepening depression.

He found, through the Wall Street Journal, an old retired city newsman who had always dreamed of living in Colorado, and a pretty good deal was made.

The new owner, not in the least mechanically inclined, also lacked knowledge of business problems.

He sat in the big swivel chair by the old roll-top desk, smoked cigars and read western magazines for some time before he realized that the paper was producing more bills than checks.

I called his attention to what appeared to me to be an inequity by showing him that I was doing over 30 hours per week in work and was still getting only the $2.50 my father had allotted me.

He invited me to sit down and discuss the matter further, then proceeded to show me that - even though I worked harder than he did - his losses were so heavy that I was making about $100 more each week than he was.

We settled for a fifty-cent raise.

This was during the period when it was not uncommon for bank presidents to shoot themselves or jump out of tall buildings. I graphically remember, in that one little town, of two such instances where people in a position of trust chose this quick way out to the alternative of facing their lifelong friends - whose savings had been entrusted to them. Both used pistols. There weren't any tall buildings.

My father, with his bills paid and a little cash left over as a result of the sale of the Ledger, was working on an invention.

Just as he had spent about the last nickel on a model, he happened across the fact that an almost identical machine had been recently patented and was in use in Denver.

Now what?

He explained his situation to the local jeweler who was one of the two Jews in town. They were about the only ones who had any cash.

(Here I must add the fact that the other Jew was the junk dealer named Pitter and that his son, a classmate of mine, was a very popular and well-liked lad whom everyone called Jupiter and who would do Spanish translations for a nickel a page. Pitter and son made a bundle when the war came).

How can I avoid digression when there is so much to tell and so little time to spend?

Anyway.

Dad had run across an ad in the newspaper trade journal announcing the Sheriff's Sale at Auction of a newspaper on the Gulf Coast of Texas - near Houston.

He got, from the jeweler, what would have been known in earlier years as a "grubstake," to finance the trip to Texas and the effort to get the local bank to loan him enough money to buy the paper.

This was in the summer of 1931, and it was as if the whole world had come to a standstill.

Texas City, Texas, was the mainland from which the causeway went to Galveston Island. It was a wonderful deep-sea port at the mouth of the Houston ship channel.

The ship channel was not as deep as now, so that most ships bringing cargoes from Houston would stop in Texas City to "top-off." Including all this tonnage made it the sixth largest seaport in the world at that time.

The newspaper office was over-equipped with a nearly new Linotype machine and the best flatbed press any of us had ever seen. The Linotype machine, itself, had cost just over $5,000 three years before.

My father visited with the banker - who held the mortgage on the property - and convinced him that, with his wife and sons, he could make a profitable business of it. Father, of course, pointed out that such a fine city badly needed a newspaper. He showed him that he had a couple of hundred dollars, which he would need to get started, and got the banker to agree to loan him what might be required to buy the paper at the auction sale next day. Father's opening bid of $2,000 was the only one to be made and we were back in the newspaper business.

Only two of the older boys had made the trip down with him. After the deal was complete, we three younger boys fitted out the old 1920 Buick with the best set of tires we could find in Jupiter's huge pile and started to drive the 1500, or so, miles. We stopped in every junkyard along the way looking for more tires of our peculiar size. We consumed fourteen before reaching our destination.

That's one thing that's better now than in the "good old days" - probably because Congress or Ralph Nader never got involved with tires.

Brother John had just finished high school and had no hopes for college in such a chaotic financial situation.

Dad had the answer though.

As he'd rummaged through the desk he found the papers that had come with the Linotype machine. Included was provision for the one chosen to operate it to attend the factory school in New Orleans, with all expenses paid. This, alone, was worth the major part of the $2,000 that Father had paid for the entire business and all the equipment.

Operating one of these things was a comparatively simple procedure, which could be "picked up" in a few weeks. But, to be able to make all the thousands of adjustments and repairs was a trade few had mastered. Brother John, though a diabetic, made a lifetime career of it after joining the powerful Typographical Union. At one time he, his wife, and all four of his children were attending the University of Arizona.

This may seem like quite a digression now, but I'll get back to it later.

———————

I worked there, much as in Longmont, before and after school while I did my senior year - but I also found time for football, track, and tennis.

What sticks out in my memory is the long process of hand-feeding several thousand blotters with the pictures of "THE WINNERS - HOOVER and CURTIS," which my father never found any use for. He and the soon-to-be ex-postmaster were the only Republicans in town.

This tended to hurt a little, as the Brain trust took over, and he soon got the urge to advertise the rejuvenated newspaper for sale - again, with a well-written ad in the Wall Street Journal. The positive approach of the ad brought out all the good, but didn't mention the odor of petrochemicals and refineries in the area or its vulnerability to coastal storms.

A former editor of the World Book Encyclopedia called by phone, settled the price at $8,000, and said he would drive down, be there in a few days.

Now we have to go back a little.

The previous year a humdinger of a hurricane had lifted the roof from a building across the street and smashed it through the boarded up (in anticipation of the storm) plate glass windows of the building in which the newspaper was located. (The rent was

$30 a month and the other three rooms in this square business block were empty.) It was necessary to post a watchman until repairs could be made. The cost of this, along with an estimate of the repairs, accompanied Dad's letter, in lieu of a rent check, to the absentee owner somewhere in Michigan. Soon the owner was on the phone wanting my dad to make him an offer to buy the building.

Father told him, truthfully, "If you ask for $500, I don't have it."

"Get it and you've got a building," was the quick reply.

Dad went to the same banker, told him the deal, and borrowed another thousand - so he could use half of it to repair the building.

He, then, leased the choice room the newspaper had occupied to the public service company, for $100 a month on a two-year lease, and moved the newspaper to the less desirable room next door. The smaller room he rented to a struggling young dentist - and took most of the rent out in dental work for our family of 10. A much less desirable room, on a totally empty side street, he rented to a damndemocrat with a beer license - on the theory that "It will be good to keep all the bums he might attract off the Main Street."

Now let's get back to the man from New York who had always dreamed of being his own boss. He arrived with a sharp looking wife in a new LaSalle. He'd forgotten to ask about the rent, which was $80 per month - much less than the power company paid for the corner.

His wife soon became disenchanted with the society and the smell of the refineries - which smelled like bread and butter to those whose husbands worked there.

Soon an ad appeared in the regional trade journal offering the paper for sale. He got $6,000 from a couple of capable young fellows and headed back to New York.

His dream hadn't cost too much in view of the fact that he seemed to be pretty well heeled. All things are comparative.

Dad's financial position had improved considerably, but his frugality hadn't suffered. We were, at this time, living in a $25 per month house that was almost big enough - but we had no income.

Then came quite a surprise.

A telegram from Dad's brothers in Denver.

They'd decided that their mother was no longer able to live alone and had satisfied her desire to see her other son by buying her a one-way ticket to Texas City.

She slept in a hurriedly purchased bed in the living room for several months before she passed away.

By this time Dad had about had it. His arthritic joints kept worsening, and he finally took to the same bed.

After awhile it occurred to him that he wasn't accomplishing anything there. He designed, in his mind, a building for a specific lot, called the owner of it, bought it, and had us carry him downtown each day where he could sit under an umbrella and watch the construction - of course with the banker's money.

Each two years he raised the rent on the public service company when their lease came up for renewal. They didn't like to tell people to go somewhere else to pay their bills.

He built an A&P store to their specifications on a long-term lease.

He, with my older brother doing the legwork, bought houses construction workers at the new refinery had built for themselves - usually at their asking price. He then "dolled them up a little" and sold them to the operations people - who were gradually arriving - at bargain prices compared to what they'd expected.

All told, I figure he made about a quarter of a million right in the depths of the depression, while in failing health, and without ever talking to a politician or taking advantage of anyone. Much of it is hearsay because I was away most of the time. Remember those 22 jobs I had between '33 and '36? And anyway, most of this came after that.

Now, we've got to go back again. I always had a job.

Before I was old enough for the one in the print shop in Longmont, I used to do the same as in Idaho Springs - ride with the milkman before school and run into the houses with the bottles of milk. The milkman in Longmont, when he sold extra, would pull into a particular barn, and water down the last can or so a little, so we wouldn't run out. I never asked his politics.

After that, on my way home from a Boy Scout meeting one night, I got an offer of a different kind of job for right after school closed.

It came clearly to mind a couple of years ago when I read in that huge Best Seller about Colorado, *Centennial*, that "the worst thing about sugar beets is you'd have to get somebody to thin them."

Several of us would meet on a certain corner each morning at 6:30 and wait for the truck. It stopped several places and finally had about 12 men and 12 boys in it when we left town.

The men were the choppers and the boys the thinners. The men each had a good sharp hoe and a file with which to keep it that way. The boys each had a pair of kneepads. The men's pay was set at 30 cents per hour and the boy's at 15 cents.

We would pull up at this farm - some ten miles out of town - and drive into a tremendous field of tiny seedlings that had sprouted from the carefully contoured and irrigated rows. The men would chop out all but two or three plants every 18 inches. The boys would crawl along on their hands and knees, decide which was the most likely looking of the plants that were left, then pick the others out by hand. At the end of the twelve rows - about a mile away - there was a bucket of water, a dipper and a little shade under the cottonwood trees that grew along the bank of the irrigation ditch.

After a couple of minutes of rest, we'd start back along the next rows towards where the truck was parked. The men were mostly Mexicans, and the boys were mostly classmates - kids, like me, who had nothing else to do and were willing to work for a buck. After ten hours we would pile into the truck and head home, then be ready to meet the truck at the same time the next morning.

When Friday came we had about two thirds of the field thinned out and were anxious for payday.

Our boss explained that he wanted to be sure we all showed up Monday because the job had to be finished by Wednesday night, which was when he would get paid.

When we had finished the last rows on Wednesday we noted, from the far end of the field, that our boss was inspecting the job with the owner of the place and that the two went into the house together.

We trudged up the furrow, carrying the hoes and kneepads, only to discover that the truck was gone.

After talking our predicament over with the farm owner - who assured us that he had paid the thinning contractor - the truth began to dawn on us, one by one.

We left the tools there and trudged back home.

My father took the subject up with the sheriff who quickly asked, "Did your son have a contract of any sort? What was the man's name? What was his license number?"

That was a good $15 lesson and didn't make me as sour as Dad was on Democrats - yet.

In fact I still think that some of the things Roosevelt did were right. This is said, charitably, in spite of the fact that one of his first moves was to cost me my job and seemingly kill any chance I had of going to college. That'll come a little later, though.

Then I went to work for the canning company - who bought the yield of a string bean field "where it stood" and arranged for their own pickers. The pay was 54 cents per hundred pounds. I would eat a 25-cent lunch while picking enough to earn 50 cents. Mexican families with plenty of kids could make a living at it.

While I was still in high school in Texas, and after my Dad had sold the paper there, I worked for the brief new owner.

One specific recollection should be recorded. There was a serious challenger to the long-established County Sheriff, who had allowed the Mafioso of the times to run a "wide open" Galveston as sort of a playground for tourists, sailors and hell-raisers from Houston. (Something like what Atlantic City promises to become.)

The Quixotic challenger had written some explosive things about this condition and wanted them circulated - though no newspaper would touch them.

He'd brought them into our mainland printing plant to be printed in newspaper form. He ordered 10,000 copies - which meant a ten-hour press run on our big flatbed press.

I was elected to feed the press - which meant flipping the sheet just right so it could be floated on a layer of air over to the guide pins. It was the sort of monotonous job - which has been practically eliminated from all sorts of industry - but one had to mind his business and couldn't be looking around while the press was going.

The candidate had gotten word, through his grapevine, that the sheriff was going to send people over to see that the publication never got printed. He locked all the doors, laid a pistol across his lap, and sat right behind me that whole Friday night - just in case. Not everyone's Gramps ever faced a situation just like that.

Why should I record this 45 years after the fact? Simply to note that there were, are, and presumably will be, the good guys and the bad guys - ready to do battle over most anything.

The ritual of high school commencement (or graduation) was much the same then as it always was and always will be. Some had a feeling that they were through learning - others had the same sort of feeling that they were about to start. That's why homogenization doesn't work.

I chose to try to figure some way to go to college, and as a starter, hitchhiked to Colorado to visit my brother who had one more year to go. He had an apartment with two other students who had gone for the summer, so I just moved in and started looking for a job somewhere in Boulder.

The only one that seemed to be available was at an all-night lunch counter known as the HALF A DIME, which was one of several owned by a man in Denver. It was right on the fringe of the Colorado University campus and did a big business, based on price, when college was in session. During the summer business was mighty slack, especially in that summer of '33.

The name meant just what it said - anything on the menu was 5 cents. This included, one pan cake, one fried egg, a hamburger, a malted milk, a bowl of chili, a bowl of soup, a glass of milk, etc. , etc., even to a ham sandwich or an ice cream cone.

Two of us worked the night shift 7 P.M. to 7 A.M. The manager (an ex-marine with a wife and four kids at home) got $20 per week - I got $5. On a busy weeknight we did well to take in more than $10. On some Saturdays we went over $20. In addition to the cash we were paid we got our meals and cigarettes. I, of course, started smoking, to squeeze a little more out of the job. My boss interpreted this fringe benefit to mean food for his family too. When things got real slack, around midnight, he would pack enough grub for the lot of them and have me walk up to his apartment and wake up his family and help his bedridden wife feed the kids. I would note, on return, that the register hadn't advanced - whether there were dishes to wash or not.

Roosevelt was starting to get in operation. Long lines formed at the banks each day in hopes that they might open.

I had put in some five weeks in this diner where we doubled up morning and evening - during the rush and in order to eat - and hadn't had a day off yet. The Brain Trust, which had been hastily assembled in Washington, killed the job. They ruled, through the short-lived National Recovery Act, that minimum pay for this industry must be 30 cents per hour. Mine was, effectively, five cents.

The only option left to the owner was to eliminate my position. With no job and nothing to eat, I bid my brother and my dreams of college a fond farewell, picked up my little suitcase and headed for the highway to "thumb" my way home. The $25 I had earned was almost intact because I hadn't had time to spend any.

Even though I had enough money to eat and sleep I canvassed each newspaper in each town along the way. I worked a couple of days in several of them, just to help the owners get caught up but didn't run across a spot with any permanent promise.

When I got back to Texas, it was the middle of August and I heard they were hiring out at one of the refineries - the pay was 65 cents an hour!!!

One of my old high school girlfriend's brother was doing the hiring, so I was one of a dozen or so chosen out of probably 200 who responded.

The job turned out to be temporary and tough.

Some of those big 80,000-barrel tanks that make up a tank farm were to be thoroughly cleaned so they could be used for gasoline storage.

The first project was to dig a big hole (40 feet long, 10 feet deep, and 20 feet wide) in the swamp outside - adjacent to one of the riveted plates that made up the tank.

Then we - the 12-man crew - chiseled the rivet heads off the bottom plate of the tank and brought in a crane to remove it.

Then we discovered, as a preliminary to the cleaning, that the tank had been filled with steam for three days and there was a foot of heavy black sludge inside. A little oozed out into our pit.

Then we were provided with a v-shaped scraper with four handles on it. Four of us would wade in through the warm goo, set the scraper down, and a cable from the gasoline winch would pull it out. We continued this for several days - working our way further and further into the back of the tank. At each distance there was more heat and less air. It was a welcome relief to "take a break" and sit in the August sunshine of the Texas Gulf Coast and sweat instead.

Then, with pick and shovel, we chipped out the half-inch or so of asphalt that had been laid prior to the first filling with crude oil.

Then we erected, inside, a scaffold on wheels - seven men high - and proceeded to wash down the tank with kerosene. Being the youngest, I was left on the floor - so the six above could drop their kerosene on me.

After several days of this we were nearing the end of the chore. The bottom of the tank had been built stronger with two steel plates. We cleaned the joints, where they were butted together with long wires with rags tied to them.

Another gang laid new pipes to and from the tank, while we steam heated the sludge in the pit, pumped out what we could, and interred the rest of it.

I've often wondered how they can do it any differently now. Surely someone must still work.

————————

Now it was full-season on the cotton docks, and sometimes there weren't enough union men to fill all the jobs at the 7 A.M. "shape up."

A couple of buddies and I would go down and hope to get picked for a gang. The gang got paid, under union contract, based on how many bales they put aboard a ship. Each member of a good gang could earn as much as a dollar an hour - if they all hustled. The hustle was the responsibility of the "gang-pusher."

When we failed to make connections there, we would go over to the, non-union, salt dock which, very wisely, started at 8 A.M.

Here, there would be eight freight cars full of nitrate fertilizer shunted onto the dock on both sides of a big moving belt that rose at the end so that it was over the hold of a ship.

There were six men and a pusher assigned to each gang. It was like a race. We all unsealed the cars together and, for the first few minutes, simply shoveled the "salt" out. Then we used wheelbarrows. This stuff had a tendency to harden up like rock salt if it got damp and we frequently loosened it up with a stick of dynamite, then used picks and shovels to load the wheelbarrows.

There was a water boy who made his rounds with a bucket and a dipper, and we all took a half-hour break at noon. Each gang member got thirty cents per hour except for the pusher - who got thirty-five. The first gang to empty their car, would not only get the pride of victory but the knowledge that their pusher got an extra five cents per hour. I never did think this was quite fair. The other thing I didn't think was quite right about it, was that we got paid off in cash on Saturday morning - in a beer joint.

As a digression it must be pointed out that this stuff, which we handled so casually, was what, in the late forties, created one of the greatest disasters of all time. A ship filled with it exploded - killing hundreds and destroying blocks. It showered my dad, over two miles away, with broken window glass but didn't scratch him.

So I'm not anti-Roosevelt. These were the kinds of situations he was trying to correct - with his Brain Trust.

––––––––––

Then I got a job in a garage. The owner was a first-class mechanic. He had a lot of fine equipment for overhauling engines and completely rebuilding cars. Junking a car was unheard of. How would you buy another? I did little details like sandblasting spark plugs and resetting the gaps.

Now they just throw them away.

––––––––––

Then I took over a filling station my older brother had talked Father into leasing for him.

When Father came down to check it out and found a rap game going on in the back room - and no money in the till - I took over.

It was a Conoco Station in a town where practically everyone worked for a refinery of one kind or another - and there was no Conoco. My customers were sparse.

The Mayor would come in and charge a tankful.

Another car would drive off before I even got its license number.

A real hustler offered to solve all my problems by bringing a string of customers to get their cars polished . He would demonstrate his product down where the action was, then lead the customers to the source of supply. I bought a couple dozen bottles of his polish in preparation for the rush.

Kids learn slow.

Then the Spring thaws loosened up the Great Lakes shipping - which made more desirable jobs available to the seamen of the ships that hit our port. There were vacancies. This was about the time that Grandmother arrived, and I decided to go see the world again so the house wouldn't be so full and the food would go further. (Incidentally, Grammy used to say, after a cursory look at the newspaper, "I've read enough of killing and violence - will you please get me my bible.")

I told my mother I was leaving that evening - but actually I was to report to the ship at 4 A.M. Some of my buddies came to see me off - with a fifty-cent pint of "rot-gut."

I spent about four months on this tanker as an ordinary seaman (at $40 per month) running to all sorts of Gulf Coast and Atlantic seaboard ports before she finally hit her home port of Philadelphia.

I could bore you with a lot more detail on this but will stick to two memories that stand out.

One was rounding the tip of Florida and looking at the "million dollar sparrow roosts" - the steel frames of hotels that had been dreamed up and financed before the crash. Most of them - even though I presume they paid for themselves after completion - are in deep trouble again.

The other memory was preparing for entering homeport after such a long stay away from it.

In spite of the rough seas (to which we had become accustomed) around Cape Hatteras, it was deemed necessary to repaint the fancy stripes on the smokestack. It was a long job and had to be started as soon as possible. I was hanging in a bosun's chair at the top - working my way down. The further down I got, the further out I swung as the ship rolled. It got to where about two licks with the brush was as much as I could do before losing contact.

The Port Captain was proud of the way the ship looked.

I wonder how they do it now?

———————

When we got in port, the Great Lakes had frozen again, so all those union cardholders were available, which left me astray in Philadelphia.

I soon got a berth as pantry man on another tanker - some Filipino had been cut with a razor. My job was almost identical to that of the men in the S2 Division of the Navy. I cooked breakfast completely. Made salads, etc. to go with the main courses, from the galley, for the other meals. I kept the coffee coming and took care of the rooms of half of the officers. The waiter, or Steward, took care of the other half.

You ask how did I know how?

He showed me one morning.

———————

I could go on and on with all sorts of detail and all sorts of jobs not worth mentioning.

Grandmother had passed on to her reward, and there was room for me at home again.

———————

Then we come to Curly Gripp.

He had a contract with the contractor who was building a tremendous new refinery in Texas City. What he needed, instead of the contract, was a lawyer and an accountant. He loved trucks and knew how to fix them and thought he knew what it cost to operate them. He had a friendly banker (some of whom were still around).

Curly's contract was with the subcontractor who was doing the concrete work.

It called for Curly to furnish Ford dump trucks with drivers "as needed" at one dollar per hour.

I got in on the ground floor - with the first dozen or so.

Each truck was equipped with a gate, set at a measured distance in the bed so that a proper mix of sand and gravel could be dumped, along with cement and water, into the huge mixers at the site. The immense piles of sand and gravel were at the rail siding. A mechanical bucket loaded sand into the truck. Then a gang of men shoveled in the proper amount of gravel. Then drivers, such as I, would head wherever we were told and back into the mixer. It was all very simple - except... the clay and the ruts of the Gulf Coast subsoil wreaked havoc with the trucks.

Curly worked all night, most every night, replacing clutches and transmissions and spent most of his days in Houston junkyards looking for more.

In view of his problems, we didn't feel it too unfair that we weren't paid our thirty cents an hour for the time that the truck was "down." That meant we fixed flat tires for nothing, greased the vehicle each morning, and washed it each evening - all on our own time.

I finally got the call from my brother in Kansas that I mentioned earlier. Curly had no trouble replacing me.

So, this is a hearsay digression. When the job was finally finished, Curly had 100 trucks in various states of decay (which the bank repossessed), a set of divorce papers from his wife, and a motorcycle.

I promised that there were 22 different jobs, and there were, but most aren't worth mentioning this long later. So, to make up for the skipping of the others we'll make the last two into one - because I had the same boss for both.

After I felt that the costs of living in Kansas exceeded the pay that Boozie offered, I hung my thumb out again - as before, stopping several places along the way as a regular "tramp printer."

I finally stopped in a little east Texas town, where there was a man with more problems than I had. He wasn't much older, either.

He'd recently concluded that a county seat town like this needed a newspaper, and he decided to start one. He'd been sold a lot of junk at a very low price and was trying to meet the post office deadline every week.

The typesetting machine was a Model 5 Linotype - workhorse of the industry and, in proper condition, completely capable of meeting his needs.

The newspaper press was from the Civil War. It had been designed to be driven by hand power. (My dad told me later, "We used to get a big "coon" and give him a swig of beer when he got thirsty and he would crank out enough for most any small paper.") This press had been modernized to increase the speed. A 2x4 with a big spiral wire spring had been added to each end - to help the bed move back and forth. Then a belt had been put on to the flywheel and attached to a big electric motor. It ran pretty well in warm weather, but when it got cold we had to put coffee cans full of burning gasoline under the ink plate before it would run.

We also had the problem of power supply. After a couple of times shutting off all the lights in town by pulling the switch and overloading the system, we learned to get the tender of the town's generating plant (a lone diesel engine) out of the barroom, to stand by before we started the run.

By now I'll bet that most of you think this is fiction, but it isn't.

Let me describe my room. It had a pot under the bed and every morning the landlady came in with a fresh basin of warm water.

Our "newspaper plant" was directly across the street from the county court house - but actually very remote. There was no semblance of paving or even street surfacing - simply sand that you would sink into at least six inches if you took a step.

We had no way to publish pictures or cartoons but one day a sample came in the mail. It was a piece of metal coated with chalk. If a drawing were scratched into the chalk and down to the metal, it would become a matrix against which we could pour molten lead in our casting machine. The boss tried it out by drawing a picture of one of the county commissioners getting bogged down in the sand - on the way to the post office with the request for government funding, which was available for paving the square. Many of us thought it was a reasonable request.

Anyway, I'm digressing again.

The idea is to show you why I left this job.

I'd had enough experience now to make most any typesetting machine work for me. I had tried them all. The one in Longmont was a Linograph, the one in Kansas was an Intertype; all the others along the way were various models of Linotype. This one, though, that had been bought (maybe even from the fourth owner), simply dropped off the truck and hooked up to electricity. It wouldn't do the job we needed - for me. It was too much worn and too much out of adjustment.

I called my brother John who had gone to the factory school.

This left me without a job.

The boss got a bright idea. Somehow he'd gotten, in the deal, an old mailing franchise and almost no equipment. This was in an even smaller town about fifteen miles up the road - halfway between Houston and Dallas.

John now had our Linotype working fine, and we knew enough to call the man before we started the press. Why not expand?

I became editor of the Buffalo Press - on commission. If it prospered, I would. This was still 1935 and advertising didn't do much good. People knew what they wanted and just worried about paying for it. All the countryside would gather on Saturday, buy pink lollipops for the kids, swap yarns, and get their sowbelly and beans to go with the greens they already had at home.

I sold a few subscriptions but had to use the money from them to pay the landlady. (Incidentally, this was a different sort of rooming house. It had the pot under the bed and the basin of water but it had only one heating stove. That was in the schoolteacher's bedroom).

I would gather what news I could - which was near nil - and send it by bus down to Centerville, the county seat, where it would replace a little of the other paper and come back to me with a new masthead - just as if I'd done the whole thing (unless you stopped to think). I got to be pretty popular around town and things started to move a little. We formed a Lion's Club and I was vice-president. Nearly everyone chipped in with a little ad for our special Christmas Edition, but it was obvious, by then, that the thing wouldn't work.

I told my friend - never Henry or H.B., always Mr. Fox - when he gave me my $8 for the week, that I better be on my way and forget about Buffalo. I told him I knew one of the local residents who'd take on the editorship.

H.B., as I call him now, was no run of the mill, all-for-one sort of a guy. He was curious about where I might go and what I might find there and wanted to chat a little.

We ended up by packing my beat-up suitcase, our two bodies, and my $8 into his old car for a little "drive." Just as we got started on the two hundred-mile drive to Georgetown, in Central Texas, where he had gone to college, it started to snow. This wasn't totally unheard of - maybe two inches a year fell in that area.

Halfway there, I edged up to a portable gas heater in a gas station where we had stopped, and burnt a little round hole in my only "good" pair of pants.

We didn't talk much. He still doesn't. His book, *The 2,000 Mile Turtle and Other Episodes from Harold Smith's Private Journal,* copyrighted in 1975 (forty years later) - twice excerpted in the *Reader's Digest* and acclaimed in newspapers from Los Angeles to Boston as "having the flavor of Mark Twain and Will Rogers," being good for a "laugh a line," "pricked with satire and sparkling humor..." etc. - was only 128 pages.

He'd graduated, only a few years before, from this Methodist college - Southwestern University - where we were headed. He had a few suggestions to make. There were a couple of fellows there who might be able to steer me right so that I could get elected to a job on one of the publications. He continued, "You might have to take up with one of these fraternities, but I don't see any sense in paying some guy in New York $50 so you can shake hands with your roommate." Three and a half years later, at graduation, I was President of the Pledges. My buddy, Tom Barton, who became a milkman in Houston and who I'll mention again later, was the only other senior in the fraternity. He was also still a pledge. People understood that $50 was a lot of money.

But I've digressed again. We've got to go into a little detail as to what happened during those three and a half years.

My friend stopped in front of the Bible professor's house and rang his doorbell. Mr. Fox introduced me, told the nice looking (and very old looking) man that I wanted to go to college, and that maybe I could sleep in his upstairs room and mow the lawn - when the time came - to pay for it.

Mr. Fox then suggested I stop by the business office of the school next morning and see what I could work out. Then he abruptly left for the long ride - all alone - back to his own problems.

This was during the holiday mid-term break, and we had time to get a grade transcript from my old high school in Texas City. While I was waiting I went to work for a newly established newspaper to get enough to eat and buy some presentable looking clothes.

When school reopened I had a place on the payroll of the National Youth Administration - another good idea that Roosevelt had before the Brain Trust smothered him. It would help to pay my tuition. The office had also written concerning a Masonic scholarship for which I seemed to be eligible.

I wanted to get in good and solid before telling my parents about this opportunity - as things were at the bottom for them, and I didn't want another disappointment - so I'd been there about six weeks before I wrote them.

I'd never found time to study English grammar in all the various schools I attended and, on testing, was found to be in need of "zero" (no credit) English. The class met while I was working at the newspaper, and the test came at a particular time when I just couldn't leave the publisher in the lurch. The nifty-looking daughter of the department head was the instructor for this course, and she arranged for me to take the exam in the evening at her home. I passed.

My room worked out great, but food was a problem. The only source for me was in town - a mile away - where cash was required. The next year there was an innovation on campus - a "new" dormitory for low-budget freshman students. It was a big, old house that was equipped with bunk beds and four study tables to a room. A retired minister operated it with his wife and sons. They bought the food, did all the menu making, cooking, and serving themselves. The cost was less than half that at the other dormitories. There were, I believe, thirty residents.

My political advisors quickly noted the need for an "honor council" for this new hall, and I was soon president of it.

The National Youth Administration (NYA) had, in true governmental fashion, made jillions of rules and regulations. Some sort of complicated formula told the college how many hours of government-supplied student labor (at 30 cents per hour) they were entitled to, and these hours were allotted, according to need, to the participating students. "Scotty," the business manager made certain that he got his full allotment from Uncle Sam.

Many of the students who had signed up were too busy, either studying or enjoying life, to work the full number of hours allowed them. As a result there was little similarity between the hours turned in for individuals by their local supervisors and the hours Scotty reported to Washington. No one ever saw Scotty's check. Student checks were handed out through the cage face down so the student could endorse the back.

Professors, who were getting paid only one month out of three - and hanging on because there was no place to go - had the option of having some of this student labor paint and paper their (college provided) housing, in lieu of money they weren't getting anyway. They would frequently give credit for double or triple hours to a deserving student who did a good job. I got several of these.

I finally landed in the reserve library as foreman of the bookbindery (which bound magazines into volumes). The librarian seldom showed up, so I also took over as reserve librarian. Then there was a vacancy in the job of writing publicity articles for the school. I took that too. So, I was doing three jobs at once from the same desk and getting ninety cents per hour (applied toward my tuition).

A young politician named Lyndon Johnson was appointed by the Roosevelt Brain Trust to administer this program for the state of Texas. When one of his bird dogs reported to him that there was a guy at Southwestern doing three jobs at once, he came to see. After a brief explanatory chat, in which I showed him that I could legitimately handle all three jobs at once, he gave me a pat on the back and went on his way.

We don't want to drag this sort of stuff out too long - just a few more little tales.

As part of Hell Week at the fraternity house each pledge was required to acquire a farm animal and stake it in the front yard. We had one out-of-state student in school - a kid we called Jeep who had, for some reason, wandered down there from Rochester, New York. When an irate woman called the police in hopes of finding her milk cow (which she did), the police asked Jeep if he'd stolen it. He quickly and unconsciously said, "No. I stole the goat over there."

There was the time that a young couple was surprised, in a practice room in the Fine Arts Building late in the evening, when the Dean of Music unlocked the door and turned on the lights in search of something he'd left there. He made a hurried retreat and next day mailed the young lover a note asking him to drop by his office. His remonstration was, "Young man, I just wanted you to know that there's no hard feeling between us. I presume you realize that it is my duty to frown on that sort of conduct."

The hall where I spent the first year, was turned into a football dormitory - with training table - as part of an all-out effort by the coach and his followers to turn out a winning team.

A young lady from the country, who had been smuggled in by one of the players, took a liking to the place and spent three days there. That became an open secret. It was a shock, when I took over the seventh grade history class in the Georgetown Junior High for practice teaching, to see this smiling young face among those who greeted me.

College hasn't changed much - in a lot of ways.

It was a "dry precinct," but there was a beer joint within six miles in all four directions.

Most of the students had no idea what was involved in the jobs of editor and business manager of the yearbook, the magazine, and the newspaper, and few had much interest.

Each of these publications was included, as a must, for each student - in other words, the cost was written into the overall tuition and fees.

Those who were selected by ballot to edit and manage them were, in effect, fully subsidized entrepreneurs - responsible only to the college business manager. In other words, the ads we sold were all profit and there might be some savings in the publication costs besides. I became business manager of the magazine for the second full year I was there. It was only natural to ask my old benefactor to bid on its production. Sure enough, he was low bidder and gave us excellent service.

The next year I was business manager of the yearbook, and my campaign manager's father got the contract. (My old friend couldn't have handled it.)

That year I decided to buckle down, after figuring out that by taking a couple of extra courses and a correspondence course I could make up for the half-year I missed at the beginning, and graduate in three and a half years.

By graduation day I had all my bills paid and a couple hundred dollars in my pocket.

Others had noted rumblings of war, some had made demonstrations.

There had been such asinine suggestions as holding a referendum before war could be declared - and sending all those who voted for it first. There was even some sort of a hunger strike. I was simply too busy for this sort of thing.

A week before graduation I got a letter from a complete stranger, down in East Texas, asking me to join his staff in a growing chain of weekly newspapers. This was a most interesting little town in several ways. It was the perfect example of the fact that people don't like to be homogenized.

There were only two kinds of East Texans - Methodists and Baptists. (That is, of course, discounting the dark folks who lived in their own community at the end of town and only came shopping on Saturday mornings.)

There was a bank for Baptists and one for Methodists.

The same with lumberyards.

The same with grocery stores.

The same with dry goods stores.

Generally they were divided like the churches were - one on each side of the railroad tracks.

I was steered to the Methodist boarding house, where a county commissioner and the football coach lived, in a nice new $3,500 FHA house, with an elderly couple.

The master of this opulence could afford it because he was the "sawyer" in a "company town" saw mill about eight miles away. He got $12 a day for keeping all the saws sharpened and in top-notch condition. Most every one else there got $2.97 - the minimum wage of $3.00 for ten hours, less the one per cent Social Security. They didn't get paid in cash though. They were paid, daily, in scrip, which was accepted in the company store for rent payments, etc. When one accumulated $10 worth of scrip, he could exchange it in the company office for cash.

But, we're digressing again.

The point was that this man could afford a new house and a car to go back and forth to work, not only because he got four times the normal pay, but because his frugal wife took in boarders. She provided us with some sort of 7-steak, beef stew, brains and eggs, or similar fare, every meal, but stuck to the local diet of sowbelly, beans and greens herself. The charge for room and board was $7.00 per week.

When she knew (through the grapevine, I guess) that I had a date with a Baptist Sunday School teacher, she was waiting up for me. We had a little heart to heart discussion over the problems that might arise from "getting mixed up with the wrong kind of people."

That was the summer of 1939, and there was a distinct understanding that there was to be no discrimination.

———————

That was in the days of W. Lee O'Daniel, ex-Governor of Texas, who was running for the U.S. Senate - so he could go to Washington and "twist the tails of those professional politicians." He was going to enact a "transactions tax" which, I figured, would hit the oil producer once, but the purchaser of a loaf of bread about 13 times. It didn't seem very democratic to me, and I pointed this out in my little column in the newspaper. I also made mention of the situation over in the company town (which company, incidentally, sent us all their job printing without asking for price quotations). Then I discovered that the fellow who had hired me had a silent partner, who was to later become Governor of the State of Texas. My only efforts in the field of politics had fallen on non-appreciative ears.

Just about then - I never knew whether by chance or by design - I was offered a far better job as, what would now be called an "account executive," but then was known as a "traveling salesman."

I was to call on all the weekly newspapers between New Orleans and El Paso. There were about 300. My main objective was to sell "ready-print." Such was used by about 20 per cent of them. We would, in Houston, print the newspaper name, date, and page numbers on four pages of features - columns, crossword puzzles, comics, cartoons, and ads - mostly for patent medicines. We would, then, ship the required number of sheets to the local paper, which would put local news and ads on the other four pages and have a double-sized newspaper for the same amount of work. The charge was little more than the cost of the paper because our company collected, on a nationwide basis, for all the advertising we thus placed.

Most editors were set in their ways about such service, and the goal was to simply maintain the business we had - in other words - to find another customer about as often as we lost one.

We also sold every type of supply or equipment a newspaper might use.

For this job I bought a used Chevrolet (on credit, of course) and put 50,000 miles on it the year before Pearl Harbor beckoned me into active duty.

I sold it, quickly, for slightly more than I had paid for it.

Right after V-J day, the letters started coming from this ex-employer - painting beautiful plans for the future. I have, only naturally, often wondered.

After the War

The choice had been made long before.

There are many things about living on the Gulf Coast of Texas which do not have the appeal of either Boston, or San Francisco, or Denver.

My pregnant wife had moved there when our oldest son began to be too evident to suit the taste of her skipper in Maine. She was given a medical discharge, along with her Certificate of Satisfactory Service. She'd lived with my sister (whose husband was on a sister-ship carrier in our same task force) until little Norman, Jr. was born — 2 days before our first wedding anniversary, on June 7, 1944. The ants had eaten a new dress Jean had bought — and worn only once in the stifling heat. The baby developed a heat rash immediately. Little details like this, along with the strangeness of the language and the odors from the refineries and chemical plants, had prompted Jean to arrange for a train ride back to Yankee land, as soon as she felt the little guy was old enough to stand the trip.

I've only been able to get her back there once since.

She had, perhaps, oversold me a little on the prospects and possibilities of the catering business, but that was where I was to spend the next 20 years.

As I said before, the petrochemicals smell like bread and butter to those whose people work there.

After years of concentrated study at bettering the environment, a tremendous expansion in the use of air-conditioning, the location, there, of NASA, those damndemocrats in Massachusetts, and other such things, the population of Texas is growing more than five times as fast as that of Massachusetts.

I didn't have a suit of civilian clothes and was amazed to find I couldn't buy one — millions of GIs had gotten home before I did.

About one of eight in the entire population had been in uniform - to the tune of sixteen million. Perhaps four million stayed in. The rest were looking for clothes, jobs, housing, food, etc., all at once — I mean, within a year.

There was lots of adjusting to be done before disruptions of the war would really end.

The bread and butter of the catering business was the employee cafeteria at the Ford assembly plant in Somerville, a Boston suburb. The Ford plant had turned out all manner of rolling stock for the services and was now converting to Fords to supply a tremendous market that had developed during the past four years. There were a couple of other cafeterias — one in a college and one in an electronics plant. Besides that we did banquets and weddings on nights, Sundays, and holidays.

Stafford's Inc. fleet of trucks

I got ten minutes behind schedule my first day and stayed there for twenty years.

———————

During the next fifteen years we had seven more children and many asked how I found the time. I told them, "It doesn't take long!!!"

In the meantime, people used to look quizzically at my wife with such a brood and she would say, "No. I'm just a careless Protestant who loves kids."

Norman Sr. holding Vicky, Jean, Norman Jr., Norma, Arthur, Ronnie, Judy, Kim - 1958 (Candee was born 1959)

We got one of the first television sets. It had a seven-inch screen - and a big plastic "lens filled with liquid" that would greatly enlarge the picture - from the National Radio Company. This was their first effort at conversion to a civilian market.

We would get a truly "custom made" Ford each year. My Ford plant cafeteria customers would get the job number of my new car and follow it through the line, supplying all sorts of extras in the way of welding, cushioning, paint, etc. It was amazing what a difference they could make.

It was customary, every summer, to get some kind of action to replace the weddings and banquets that didn't occur.

One day a fellow with a problem dropped in. He could get permits for the sale of ice cream and soda water on the Boston Common but didn't know what to do after he got them. He had never attempted such a thing — had no cash, credit, or contacts with which to get started.

There were thousands of people wandering around there, I couldn't see how we might miss and got enthused over the thing but was, of course, a little wary. If it was so good, why wouldn't he take it to a friend — he seemed to know everyone.

Anyway.

We sat in his lawyer's office and drew up the papers of incorporation of the Hub Concessionaires, Inc. I held thirty percent of the stock, Mike's wife (a former secretary of Mayor Jim Curly) held thirty percent, and Mike had the other forty. He was the Treasurer and made the deposits.

I arranged with my prime ice cream supplier to make some cute little stands on rollers — as specified in the permit. This, of course, took time. In the meantime we got regular vending boxes like they use in the ballpark - from the Pepsi Cola Company. We kept one of my waitresses busy bagging peanuts and went right in business.

It was hectic. The money rolled in — at least the part of it that I was able to shake out of the pockets of the nondescript group of sales people we had.

Mike's wife was good about making deposits and paying bills but was always too busy to make any sort of a statement to show how we were doing or to even pay me anything on account. Of course we had a manager who got paid. I was generally busy with other things.

When Jim Farley (sales manager for the Coca-Cola Company) heard about our venture, it became national news as he tried to cut our operation down to one stand - by a different interpretation of the terms of our license. We made <u>Newsweek</u>.

After about six weeks of operation I insisted on pinning Mike and his wife down to an accounting. He arranged for a meeting in the office of our attorney — who was doing poorly in his campaign for Governor.

After calling the meeting to order Mike, in all the majesty that his 5 feet 2 inch frame could muster, requested permission to address the group (of four). He left the padded chair, at the head of the table, and presented the gavel to me — the Vice President. He then took the floor and made a motion, quickly seconded by his wife, that the corporation dispense with the services of the Vice President & General Manager. Yep. You guessed again. The vote was 70-30 and, when the presiding officer asked advice of the attorney, he thumbed through the by-laws and discovered that such a vote required a two-thirds majority. It was, therefore, a legal vote.

Then the presiding officer was informed there was some thousand dollars in back pay due to him but that it was not immediately available because there had been "petty cash expenditures that the President was not at liberty to divulge." There was a discussion of giving me a note and I shot back with a simple, "Mike, you bastard, I'd rather have your hand-shake than your note." On that we shook hands. I heard a motion that we adjourn.

This was when I started to sour on damndemocrats.

When, a year later, I mailed him a bill for the thousand - and got back a note that "all our business was concluded at the time of our last meeting" - I got sourer.

The permits for the Boston Common were canceled by the succeeding Mayor but Mike quickly arranged to make use of the equipment, organization, and know-how he'd gotten from me - in the Metropolitan District Commission skating rinks, zoos, etc. He made a bundle. Still does, I guess.

———————

In 1951 some "kid from Harvard Business School," who reminded me of Bursie, became the new Personnel Manager of the Ford Plant. One of his first actions was to advise me that, inasmuch as there was no contract involved, no notice was needed, but I would have the rest of the week to finish up my operation there.

Bill Rosenberg (the founder of Dunkin Donuts) was taking over.

I got kind of sore at that one.

I spoke to some of my buddies at the plant who had talked me into putting union buttons on all my girls and who had occasionally borrowed a buck or cuffed a lunch. Just exactly three months later, the "kid from Harvard" called and asked me back. Mr. Rosenberg had found the operation to be "both unpleasant and unprofitable" — partly because he had a dietitian trying to explain to a 240-pound Irish union steward that potato chips were better for him than boiled potatoes.

I stayed there until they shifted the plant over for Edsel construction, then closed it.

Just a couple of short stories that show the difference in people — which is what this is really all about.

I always needed a good supply of strong backs to carry dishes in and out of banquet halls - mostly from high school - who worked at minimum wage till they found something better.

When two of these fellas came back from Korea here's how they differed. First, a brief description of each. Alvin was one of fourteen kids who lived around the corner. His father had gotten on welfare during the Depression and never worked since. Most of the older kids were on welfare now — with their families. Peter, a sharp little Italian with an engaging smile, was known as "Peter, the Pisan politician." He had lots of kinfolk's and was always hustling votes for some politician.

Each came back with a child or two (as they said, "one in the oven") and looked to me for work. I, or course, couldn't pay them what they'd need to live on. I took the few minutes necessary to call my old buddy at the Ford plant (the previous Personnel Manager — who was now at the other end of the building hiring hourly personnel) and told him I was sending these two down to apply for work.

Pete was, almost immediately, driving the cars off the end of the line.

Alvin was soon terminated because he wouldn't report to work on Mondays.

Let's go back to my old friend from the Baltimore, Pete Bonan. He never forgot his promise to do something about those terrible flats, in the West End, that had been offered to us as rentals.

He called me one day and asked me to meet him and his associates for lunch at the Ritz-Carleton. They showed me the grandiose plan for Charles River Park — which would replace this whole neighborhood with beautiful high rise apartment buildings — complete with restaurant, shopping center, and swimming pool. He figured that I, as a caterer, could get in the act in some way, such as feeding the construction workers then, perhaps, running the restaurant.

He later mailed me a letter of confirmation, with a copy to the construction superintendent, and at the same time, invited me to the groundbreaking ceremonies.

After the site had been cleared I was preparing to start operation of the portable diner I'd purchased for that purpose.

Then, I got a call from Pete — from his New York office.

"You'd better have a talk with the sheriff before you go any further with your plans. Maybe you should tell him you will buy your coffee from him."

I called the Sheriff, who had formerly operated a catering business much like ours but had, with so many political connections, no longer time to fool with such small potatoes.

His thing, now, was his coffee company — for which he was his own sales manager. He would make calls on potential clients along all the highways of the county in the chauffeur driven sheriff's limousine — with the blue light flashing on top — and come up with an amazing amount of new business. It was good coffee and I was willing.

The catering was a family business, which his sister and brother still ran, but at no where near its potential capacity. The physical plant and the equipment dwarfed mine and he would swing into action once in awhile, as he was the only democratic union caterer equipped to handle a big banquet. More about that later.

Anyway.

We discussed Pete's project and the fact that it wouldn't amount to much for quite awhile but might grow into something worthwhile. I showed him the diner I'd bought and suggested that we would need a coffee supply. Then he hit me.

"You don't get the idea! I've already promised this to another fellow and there'll be no building permit until it's straightened out. If I'd promised it to you you'd expect the same, wouldn't you?"

Of course the other fellow didn't need my diner.

Pete had nothing more to say on the subject. He wanted to get the project built. When it was time to start on the posh restaurant, Pete called me again. This was out of my field so I called Anthony Athanas. That's when I first heard about his plans to build Pier Four — which has won worldwide acclaim.

I could go on ad infinitum with stories about this very seldom thought of sort of business — and all the headaches and problems that go with it. It was, mostly, a matter of contacts and pricing — like any other business.

We soon ran across Jean's old boss again, and were invited out to his beautiful new home, to meet his new wife.

He had, by now, known me the required five years so that he could propose me for membership in the Ancient and Honorable Artillery Company of Massachusetts.

This is a very interesting group. The oldest military organization in the Western Hemisphere — established in 1638 by the King to protect the citizens from the Indians. In effect it is the forerunner of the National Guard.

Old Jim Curley always got a rise when, in his best oratory he would say, "They were invisible at war but invincible at the bar."

The charter calls for the election of officers, by popular ballots cast on the drum in the middle of Boston Common, on the first Monday of every June.

Each of these line officers, so elected, becomes a private again on the following June. Four United States Presidents were former privates. They include such an unhomogenized group as Calvin Coolidge, Jack Kennedy, Chester A. Arthur, and James Monroe.

Every Fall the group makes a "Fall Field Tour of Duty" to some foreign land in close cooperation with the State Department. They were, a few years ago, the only American Military Unit ever to be welcomed to Moscow.

In 1954 we flew to London for a twenty-minute parade, then went to Paris for a week "to recuperate." That was one of the last crossings in a venerable old Constellation - with four propellers and three tails. Ours was sold while we were en route. I was elected to position under Top Sergeant — mostly because one of my good customers had "hustled" votes for me in the Engineers' Club.

It wasn't long until he suggested I join the Engineers' Club, and even less time before he asked that I take the job as Chairman of the House Committee — to see what I could do about cutting down some of the terrific losses. These were made up by assessments to the members and brought some grumbles from those who didn't use the place.

My first report was to show that there were seven people on the payroll to serve breakfast, and there were usually only two members who ate it.

Solution to this problem would require more tact than I could muster so I put it in the lap of the man who'd asked for my help. The two customers were the Governor of the Commonwealth and the President of the Club. The other part of the story was that twelve breakfasts went out the back door to local and Metropolitan police who took care of the shortage of parking space. My friend kept the problem in his lap.

No.

This isn't really a digression. It gets around to another picture of them damndemocrats.

Each year, I guess as a reward for my services, or perhaps because they liked the food and service, the House Committee would choose my proposal for serving their annual outing (about 1500, served in a tent at a golf course).

One year the Sheriff came to the committee meeting and announced, "I want that job this year. Whatever price you have, mine's a quarter less."

Naturally we voted for him.

At the dinner the sheriff looked me up among the 1500 assembled members and guests and suggested he had a few things he'd like to show me. He took me behind the curtain, to the "kitchen," and introduced me to the Superintendent of the County House of Correction — who was supervising the job. Then he waved his arm towards another considerable group and announced that they were all guards there. With another sweep of his arm he showed me the rest of his kitchen crew, who were all inmates or, as he called them, guests. Then he quickly said, "How can you compete with a payroll like this?"

I commented, "Howard, the dinner was good — particularly, the salad. I presume it came from your garden at the jail farm?"

"Where else?" was his totally unabashed answer.

To carry the story a little further; there was a big dinner at the Armory when Jack Kennedy came to town. The Sheriff, probably the biggest fundraiser in the county, was toastmaster and, of course, caterer.

After most of the arrangements had been made there was a guard killed in an escape attempt at the lesser "holding" jail in the courthouse. The, inevitable, grand jury investigation was underway.

I wish I had a copy of the cartoon the Boston Herald came up with, showing the Sheriff stewing in the pot he was serving to himself, as host.

Fact of the matter was, a young scion of an old-established catering family, who'd gone in business for himself, had taken on the job of serving communion breakfast at his own parish church. He'd sent all the dishes and equipment down the night before and told the waitresses to report directly to the church to set up the tables. He would come, at serving time, with the prepared food. Yep — you guessed again. His alarm clock didn't go off. The girls called the shop, and getting no answer, assured the priests he must be on his way with the food. When the waiting got too intense somebody called his house, and the Holy Name Brothers went home, or to the nearest restaurant, for breakfast. This had brought on his bankruptcy sale and his engagement, by the Sheriff, as a jail guard who reported to duty in Malden (where the Commissary was) instead of Cambridge (where the jail was). It left one guard post undermanned, but left the Sheriff in a better competitive position as far as payroll went.

The fact that the sheriff was so brazen about such things helped sour me a little further on damndemocrats.

When these big dinners came up we were the only "union" caterers who could handle them. We would each make supervisors out of our own "steady" waitresses, then order the other eighty, hundred, or whatever, from the "union pool", They would, of course, scour the bottom of the barrel to fill the order and — as is true of any group of things or folks (even a case of eggs), some are better than others. When it got down to men, for kitchen help, this "union" wouldn't even make an effort. We were on

137

our own. I told you where the Sheriff got his, and that most of mine were high school boys (few of the cafeteria workers would take these jobs). The other source was Manpower, Inc. I saved a lot of book-keeping by simply buying hours of manpower from them, and letting them keep the payroll records.

The reason for this little digression is to point out one of the multitudinous problems of the Secret Service.

When Barry Goldwater was coming to address some 2,500, one of these strangers from Manpower got "stiff" an hour before time to serve and I had a couple of my men unceremoniously throw him out the back door of the cavernous armory, in which we were setting up. We later noted his jacket laying there and started to throw it out, too. There, in the pockets, were a parole card and a nifty little pistol. We threw the jacket and the card out, then handed the pistol to a Secret Service man.

I think the most I ever had on the payroll on any particular day was 200, but in one three-month period, there were 400 names.

That meant, when the Fourth of July came and the banquet season was over, at least 300 people would run down to get on the unemployment list, and my accountant would start cussing about all the paperwork involved. One more against them damndemocrats. Why should a housewife who was lucky enough to get a little extra work get paid for not having it when it dries up?

By the early sixties I'd had it. The pay for a "job" (generally about four hours) was $2.50 when I got in the business in '46. When I put the union buttons on, in '48, it went to $4.50, which (along with a free meal and what rolls and cake they could rescue) seemed good. By 1962 it had gotten to $16.50 plus more fringe benefits and less work. It was getting to the point where there would be so many bags of hidden rolls and cake that there weren't enough to set the table with, just for instance. The whole attitude had changed as women with a work ethic had worked their daughters in.

I was offered a job with a nationally known vending company, to teach them how to combine fresh food with automation. My business card said "Director of Research and Development."

It was only a short time later I discovered this meant *researching* for potential clients, and *developing* them into profitable customers.

We were the most selective, in a highly competitive field. The words of our Scottish leader were, "Always remember. We are a blue chip service, for blue chip clients who are willing to allow us to make a profit. Ask direct questions, insist on direct answers, and when you find you're wasting time, walk away. Don't waste any time, even at the start, with politicians."

I was the leading salesman - of five - for nearly all of the three years I stayed there but, as might be expected, found it difficult to get the performance to match my promises, and tended to get a little noisy about that at times. Three years later, after they'd picked my brains just about clean, they discovered they would have to spend more effort on production, less on sales, and would therefore no longer need my services.

I'd practically given my catering business to a guy who thought he had a little political clout and had been running his banquet business out of the government-owned kitchen in the IRS Building in Boston. But when the new JFK Federal Building was opened in Boston the Johnson administration awarded the food service contract to a Texas firm. The timing was perfect and my successor moved right into my spot.

I have, perhaps, compressed this nineteen and a half years so much you haven't gotten the picture but at least I got around to saying how those politicians happened to help me once - while crucifying a competitor.

Anyway, at age 49, I was adrift, with eight kids of various sizes, a big house with heavy mortgage payments, no job or prospects of one, and no salable trade or profession.

———

Jean who'd been forward looking, and didn't want to sit around drinking coffee the rest of her life, had been taking courses. At her Tufts University 25th reunion she donned cap and gown and was presented her Masters Degree and teacher's certificate — because her baby would be starting school the next year.

After a couple of phone calls concerning an ad in the paper, we decided to make a four-hour drive to Pittsfield, Maine to see the famous old Lancey House, which was for sale. Everything about the deal looked great but Jean was negative about the prospects of my being able to "swing it".

Original Lancey House built during 1820s

A few days later the owners called back, wanted to talk again on a particular day when they would be together. Jean couldn't go that day because she had an interview about a teaching job. Yep. You guessed again. I worked out the hotel deal and, she got the teaching job.

We were both committed to the deals we'd made so we decided to, temporarily, split the family and take both deals.

Norma Jean, who was nearing nineteen and had just finished Chandler School for Women (a busi-

141

ness college), Ronnie and Judy, who were both in high school, moved to Pittsfield with me. There was an excellent private high school, Maine Central Institute.

The hotel did a tremendous volume of business, compared to the size of the town and trade area, but had been losing money with a hired manager. There were three dining rooms, two bars, fifty bedrooms, and 48 employees.

Lancey House Mural Dining Room

I worked out a deal, something similar to what my father'd done years before in Texas. I took over as President (and one hundred percent stockholder) of a new corporation that owned the entire business — including $750 cash in the registers, $5,000 in accounts receivable, all the food, liquor, furniture, fixtures and, real estate - with no accounts payable a hotel in the town and didn't want to pick up the losses. They figured an outsider with some experience could run it better than their manager, who'd worked his way up from busboy.

We took over August 1, 1965. There was a big reunion (about 1,000) dinner at the school the first week, which provided us with a little working capital.

Very soon the $80 per week bookkeeper decided she was superfluous as long as Norma Jean was there. I spent most of my time in the kitchen (watching the back door) and we were soon showing a profit.

We were booked solid, well in advance, for November 1 (start of the hunting season).

On October 30 this big old wooden building, which had been built just after the Civil War and remodeled many times, began to smell of smoke. Pretty soon the sprinkler system started, one by one, to wet down the walls. Fire from the electrical setup in the basement had worked its way up through the closet under the stairs, through the pipe enclosures inside the walls, into the attic, and through the roof before any flames were visible. The 200 people in the building got out without difficulty. Most of the damage came from the 96 sprinklers soaking down all the furniture — which wasn't burning.

There was ample insurance, but it would pay only what it cost to restore the building to the condition it had been in prior to the fire. I couldn't picture restoring a three-story, wooden, elevator-less, Main Street hotel a mile from the interstate.

We paid off the mortgage, sold the lot to the grocery store behind us, held an amazingly successful auction sale of the water-damaged furniture, and brought that chapter to a close.

I was adrift again.

———————

Soon I was back in the big hotel adjacent to Boston Gardens where I'd previously arranged for an automatic coffee shop, "The Realm of the Coin." It seemed that people were too "well-heeled" to fool with the machines, when they could get service so many places around, and neither the hotel nor the vending company was happy with the setup.

The hotel needed a food service, but still wanted to avoid running their own.

Yep.

I was elected.

I designed a sort of hybrid setup that would serve a limited menu with minimal help. Even the minimal help was getting hard to find by then, because of them damndemocrats paying them more to be unemployed than a prudent operator could pay them to work.

Finally a guy, who reminded me of myself during my tramp printer, days stumbled in. He was amazingly capable.

I'd heard of another guy who might work out fine, if he was available, and drove down to talk with him.

That's when I, run off the road by an 18-wheeler, hit a concrete abutment on the super highway and spent two weeks in the hospital before I woke up. One surgeon sewed up my scalp and the inside of my mouth, and pulled a big spring - from the seat - out of my pelvis, while the other put a steel pin down my leg from my knee to the ankle. Next day they took my spleen out. A couple of weeks after I woke up, they sent me home in an ambulance to spend another six months in bed.

Norma was doing the bookkeeping on my little restaurant and everything looked fine — until the checks started to bounce.

This exceptionally fine manager was addicted to slow horses, and was, each day, leaving the duplicate bank deposit slip with Norma while he took the original, and the cash, to Suffolk Downs. She said, "Why, that bastard! If you were able to watch him, you'd expect something like that but when he does it while you're flat on your back, that's wrong!" There are still nine warrants for larceny outstanding against him, although the police know where his home is. His father simply says he hasn't seen him. I would think that they could find him.

At that time we decided to buy the Reeves House in Woburn — from the heirs of the people who'd moved in the year I was born. We still owned a big old house in Winchester, which I had labeled a "midget mansion."

Judy, Ronnie, Arthur in front of Winchester house

The Winchester house had seven bedrooms, three and a half baths, a big sleeping porch, an 18x36 in-ground swimming pool with patio and deck and a 12x28 foot inside basement room off the deck. The third floor was designed for, no longer existent, servants and, there was a buzzer under the table in the 20-foot dining room by which one was supposed to call the, no longer existent, maid. It had been built in the early 1900s by the forerunner of the modern developer. He had squeezed as many lots as possible out of an old farm and filled them at minimal cost. The result had been a big crack in the basement foundation which made cracked walls and uneven floors, a too small two-car garage (built for the cars of the day) and, an inadequate, fifty-foot street frontage.

I'd built the swimming pool, the deck, and the basement room during the 18 years we lived there, but the whole picture was not so appealing as to make it quickly salable.

Back of house showing part of deck and pool

I placed an ad in the Wall Street Journal — knowing that Winchester was a "demand" town, and that people were on the watch for bargains there.

The first (and only) response to the ad came from a fellow who sounded, in the Real Estate vernacular, like a real live one. I gave him a price, which, of course, had been omitted from the ad, when he told me that he had four kids and was coming to Harvard for four years — to get his doctorate.

He arrived, shortly after, and to my mild surprise — but not consternation — he was black. This was in 1968 and I thought such things no longer mattered. We made a deal. After he proclaimed that he was working for Time magazine, I, with all my experience, accepted his crisp one-hundred dollar bill as earnest money and took his word that his lawyer would send me another $1,900 with the signed agreement. Next day he wanted to bring his family to see the house. They were "salt and pepper". The white wife and the mulatto kids made quite a picture, to the neighbors, as they inspected every nook and cranny.

Two days later, while we were still awaiting the check from the lawyer, our nearest neighbors remembered that they had been planning, for years, to make a hedge of roses between the two properties. Work on the trellis-like fence started immediately.

After a few more days of waiting, we called our would-be buyer and discovered he "was having trouble selling his place" and had decided against making his move just now.

148

He asked me to send back his hundred dollars.

I'm sure if I'd sent it to him, he would have returned it to either _Time_ magazine, the NAACP, or whomever else it was, who was that interested in finding out whether a "colored" man could buy a house in Winchester.

Although the law said I must sell it without prejudice, it was obvious the neighbors didn't approve of that law. There were, and are, many ways around it for one who chooses to be devious. There still aren't many blacks in Winchester — or any other suburb out that way.

Just as a sidelight, do you realize over 32,000,000 laws have been passed — and, there are untold thousands of lawyers who are ready, willing, and able to by-pass most all of them.

In Utopia everyone would go along with the ten commandments and the sermon on the mount and the lawyers would have to go to work - along with the judges, and the court clerks, and the policemen, and the bureaucrats, and the prison guards, and the representatives, and senators - who, through the years, have come to be known as lawmakers or legislators.

This would create such a work force that we could forget about the energy crisis and environmental protection and do everything by hand.

But I stray from fact to theory.

Fact is, after much more searching, and at a compromisingly lower price, we found a buyer for our house in Winchester, and — after disposing of a truck load of good furniture that wouldn't fit the one we were moving to — moved "back" to Woburn, where Jean had lived as a little girl and where her younger sisters had been born.

While we owned two big houses with a minimal income, we rented the one in Woburn to a well organized "group" who were practicing for a definite appointment to "cut a platter" in New York. The house was perfect for them because it sat in the middle of three acres of land with no neighbors to disturb.

I used this time to create a real estate office in one stall of the four-car garage, and had had a carpenter working there for a week, before the building inspector appeared. I told him I realized the zoning code didn't allow an office in that zone, except as an adjunct to a home, and assured him that we would move in before the office was occupied. He insisted that, even though I was making no change in the foundation or the exterior of the building, I must come down and get a permit.

Two months passed before he wrote me a letter in which he refused to grant the permit.

He was later indicted by a grand jury for some other such shenanigan, but simply disappeared. As far as I know, the indictment was never carried out. His actions, though, were the simplest sort of shakedown, which have been par for the course for years and are, just recently, since Watergate, starting to attract the attention of the press.

The net result of my refusal to cooperate was that the place was a real eyesore until we finally moved in, spoke to the Ward Alderman, got the permit, and finished the job.

Long before this move, the City Council granted a zoning change so the Cadillac dealer could move in as my neighbor.

This move was, however, challenged by ten taxpayers from across the street, orchestrated by the self-appointed West Side Guardian, and taken to court. This was the first case for a recent, but far from youthful, law school graduate. He milked it and the ten taxpayers for four years before the permits were finally granted, my commission paid, and construction begun. The cost of this delay, to the Cadillac man and to the City, was in the hundreds of thousands, even though the result was a positive foregone conclusion.

Now we get to the villain of this piece.

Ed Gilgun was the man who so loudly proclaimed his honesty as to make one doubt it. He was a bachelor in his early 70s who had made a small fortune - locally, in real estate and insurance, and on a statewide basis, by having been "appointed to offices of trust by five different Governors."

One of his typical accomplishments had been to gain the beautiful and famous old Baldwin Mansion and cut it up into a six-family tenement. (The Historical Society has finally rescued it and restored it as a National Shrine.)

Anyway.

He, somehow, beat the Mayor who had been in office for eight years.

He talked the City Council into allotting $50,000 for use in beefing up the assessor's office. Then he replaced the salaried assessors (a retired insurance executive and a retired bank president) with a real old-timer who'd finally made captain, after service in navy engine rooms during both world wars and on into retirement, and another old-timer who had been Mayor during the mid-thirties. Neither appointee would make a move without the Mayor's explicit orders.

Then, without explaining to the Council that the man had been expelled from the Appraiser's Institute for being both incompetent and unethical (an almost unheard of action to be taken by local, regional and national boards of the Institute), he hired an "expert appraiser" at $50,000 per year, to advise them.

Figures from the Treasurer's office showed it would take a sixteen million-dollar increase in the tax base to avoid an increase in the tax rate. This was because of a lot of juggling the previous mayor had done to keep the tax rate down, because of inflation in general, and because of a new contract the teachers won in a bitter strike.

The Mayor was in a perfect position to do good for the City but, being a damndemocrat, he did exactly the opposite.

It would have been so simple to blame all the problems on the ex-mayor, give a little increase to most everyone's taxes, and use the discredited appraiser to straighten out some of the inequity that always did, and always will, exist in any assessor's office.

Instead, he simply ordered a total of sixteen million dollars be added to the valuation of all the properties owned by people who didn't live here and couldn't vote. This was on the theory that the Mayor had the Appellate Tax Court under his thumb, and that other court remedies were too cumbersome for a single company to tackle.

When the bills came out there was a real outcry. Salada Tea simply moved out. General Foods, Sylvania and a few other companies went to court on their own. It was, however, the reason for the birth of the Woburn Corporate Citizen's Association, which hired a topnotch Boston law firm to represent them.

The law firm pointed out that another suit by ten resident citizens would add greatly to the efficiency.

Another illegal practice, which had been going on for years, was to reassess every property at the time of its sale — without regard for the valuation placed on similar properties in the neighborhood.

That's how I got in the act.

The two suits were heard together and the judge immediately ruled that equity must be established by a complete revaluation of all the properties in the city and that, until such time as that had been done, all the respondents to both suits would pay taxes at half the rate at which they had been billed.

The Mayor kept billing at his rates and budgeting as if the half not paid was receivable.

No attempt to explain this to the voters was to any avail. He was reelected after two years by a margin of 7 to 1 and, two years later, by a margin of 8 to 1. He'd made those big corporations pay "their fair share" and relieved the burden from the backs of the working man.

The vote, in each election, was about half of those registered.

In other words, he was kept on by the city workers, their friends, kinfolk and neighbors.

The court-ordered revaluation was started by one of the two firms to bid for the job. Even though it was the highest bidder, it was decided by the Mayor, the fact that their main office was nearby made it worth the difference.

They took care of his friends first, then went bankrupt and left the bonding company to get the other firm to finish.

After the job was finished, a quick check against actual house sales — made a couple of months later — showed 69 percent of fair market value for one alderman and 150 percent of fair market value for one of the ten taxpayers who initiated the suit. Others were mostly between 80 and 90 percent.

Then, nearly six years and over half a million dollars in lawyers fees, appraisers fees, and court costs later, the judge finally ordered that corrected bills be mailed to all the participants in the suit.

The affect would have been devastating except for the fact that knowledgeable brokers and bankers had continued the building boom in the city, and an actual legitimate rise in the tax base, almost equal to the first phony one, had come each year. As it was, the city only had to borrow about 8 million dollars, at top interest, to bail out.

Incidentally, the advisor to the assessors, after the first year, got $250 per day to act as expert witness in court to testify as to the validity of the valuations he'd set. His friend, an ex-Mayor, got higher fees - as an attorney to assist the City Solicitor in the trials.

I've written bales of details on this subject (as a consultant for our attorneys, and in trying to get the picture properly presented in the local press). I've probably made it so brief here that it's confusing.

Anyway. Why did I write all this stuff besides just to pass time.

The point is there are good guys and bad guys and millions of shades of gray in between the white hats and the black hats.

Every question has its positives and its negatives.

Every lobbyist has his pitch and his angles.

The recent big play in the media, about a reform of ethics, is mostly rhetoric.

If my children's children are to get a better shake than I did, during the years of their youth, something has got to be done now to stop the plunge, which Congress seems bent on. They're as far off base as our Mayor was. It's like a microcosm.

My dentist said the other day, "I wouldn't feel so discouraged if just someone would do something right."

The people on the Hill are doing the same thing the Mayor did. They're greasing the squeaky wheel by constantly making laws that constantly keep cutting our defense potential and increasing the public debt. This went up something terrific during the waste of two wasted world wars, but has nearly tripled since 1945 — while it should have been being amortized.

What would your mortgage payment be if you refinanced your mortgage every year for all you could get?

There is no question about the fact that there are more people and more machines than there used to be. Those who are able should work at something though.

I get so fed up with newscasts and debaters who figure that defense money has gone down the drain.

It didn't go anywhere. Even the little bit that pays the active duty personnel trickles back in large amounts to the Federal till (which is long since empty).

The fuel that moves the Army, Navy, Marines and Coast Guard is (a contingent amount is kept available) bought from our probable enemies.

The CIA and the FBI have their hands tied behind their backs.

The adversaries we are bound to confront have active programs in progress to cut off at least four of the greatest strategic waterways in the world: the Panama Canal, the Cape of Good Hope, the Suez Canal, and the St. Lawrence Seaway.

To arrest further erosion of these safeguards, and to spend every dime that can be properly justified by the military (with proper supervision), seems to me to be the only American thing to do.

The money the military spends doesn't go down to the bottom of the Pacific, or rust in some field on the beach of Normandy, the way it did for years. It goes through dozens of hands — each of which adds to employment, slows inflation, and pays income taxes — while, at the same time, relieving the need for other government giveaway artists to discourage the "work ethic" by making unemployment so attractive that people prefer it.

As a simple suggestion, why not , instead of promising never to build a canal across the Isthmus of Panama, build one right now that could handle all the traffic at sea level — where it should have been in the first place — in Nicaragua. If they want to get paid for the privilege they deserve it — they have valuable property. If the Panamanian dictator wants to shout — let him!!!

I'm sure the majority of people in the fifty to eighty-year age group subscribe to this message, but it doesn't reach the right ears.

That's why, as Grampy, I'm trying to get it across to my kids in the hope that they might pass it on to some viable candidates to replace the ones we have in office now who feel that giveaway is the name of the game.

Some day, when the Golden Rule, the Ten Commandments, and the Sermon on the Mount mean the same thing to everyone, I'll be gone and, I feel, so will my kids and their kids.

Let's prepare for the foreseeable future.

THE END

Afterword

by
Norma Jean Hissong

Several years ago I gave a speech at Toastmasters about my hero, my Father-O. I've got the pages, so I'd like to include it here.

As He Lay Dying

He was thirty years old when I was born. I was forty-one when he died. The years in between were sometimes turbulent but I always knew he was my biggest fan – my Father-O. He encouraged me to believe all things are possible, and on those occasions when he had to spank or punish me, for one transgression or another, he would say, "This is going to hurt me more than it does you," and I knew he meant it. I also knew if I ever needed anything he would be the person I could count on, and I often did.

I had three brothers and four sisters, but I knew I was his favorite. To me he was the epitome of tall, dark, and handsome even though he wasn't very dark. He was about six feet two inches tall with pensive hazel eyes, short brown flat-topped hair and the straightest, whitest teeth I ever saw; so perfect that my grandfather insisted they couldn't possibly be his own, but they were. His picture perfect smile was framed by long dimples on either side, and a deep cleft in his chin.

161

He wore dark gray suits over pressed white shirts, and black wing-tipped shoes. When he kissed us good-bye in the morning he smelled of the Yardley shaving cream he applied, using a soft long-bristled brush. When he came home in the evening his "whiskas kisses" carried the scents of whatever meals he'd prepared that day in his catering business.

He enjoyed excellent health until he was in an almost fatal car accident when he was fifty years old. He suffered many lacerations and broken bones, all of which eventually healed, but his health was never good after that. He was struck with one illness and heart problem after another. Perhaps most difficult to endure was his rheumatoid arthritis, which was extremely painful, caused his fingers to become gnarled and twisted, and eventually let to replacements of a knee, a shoulder, and a hip. It was distressing when I looked up one day and realized he was no longer taller than I, but several inches shorter, due to painfully disintegrating vertebrae.

Though he was always in pain he continued to be there for me, even coming to my house to fix breakfast for about thirty people after a sunrise wedding of some friends of mine.

With all his medical problems it wasn't surprising to see relief rather than dread on his face when he was diagnosed with bone marrow cancer and told he probably had two years to live. True to form he said to me, "What can I do for you that won't take more than two years?" How could I express my sadness in light of his relief? I didn't want him to feel guilty. He could finally see an end to his pain and suffering, but I was losing my Father-O.

It wasn't two years, but only about one and a half, when I said good-bye to him for the last time – on this plane of existence.

I'd come down from Maine, as I did when I could, to visit with him and bring news and pictures of the progress my husband and I were making on the campground we were building. He always wanted to know the latest. On this day, however, he had seemingly slipped into a coma and had not been responding to anyone. A social worker arrived to discuss with some of my siblings, my mother, and me what our options were. There was a lot of talk about putting him into a nursing home, which was not something anyone wanted to do, but my mother was about at her wit's end. I felt it was a moot point because he gave every indication that death was imminent, but my mother didn't want to hear it. My sister had come from Colorado, with her three kids, to help care for Father, but she would have to leave soon. My mother became overwhelmed with conflicting emotions so my sister Judy persuaded her to go for a ride.

My sister Kimm and I stayed to look after Dad and be there when my niece woke up from her nap. Kimm got busy with some laundry. I went to sit with my sleeping father, just to hold his hand and watch him breath. When I heard Patty stirring I didn't know if I should bring her into his room or not, but decided to unless it seemed to bother him. When Patty went to the bed, stroked his face, and said "Grampie, I love you," his eyes popped open and he said he wanted to get up. Kimm and I couldn't believe our ears. It was as if he'd been somewhere far away and had just come back.

We eventually managed to get him from his hospital bed at one end of the house to his contour chair at the other. He was alert and cheerful as he sat and played with Patty.

Awhile later my mother and sister returned with a new supply of adult diapers and information on those chairs for people with no mobility, the ones that stand you up with the push of a button.

"We checked it all out," Judy said. "We can have one delivered tomorrow and Medicare will even pay for it." They thought it would be wonderful that Dad would be able to come back to the living room without having to worry about how he would get out of his chair.

As they shared their delight, Father-O's eyes clouded over and he said, "I want to go back to bed."

When he was all settled again, I asked if he wanted to see the pictures I'd brought. He said he did, but it was clear to me he wasn't really looking at them. His mind seemed a million miles away.

As I prepared to leave I said "Father-O, I love you."

He responded, "You already said that."

Suddenly I understood and I said, "Dad, what do you want?"

He wearily replied, "I just want someone to take me home to Jesus."

I said, "If that's what you want, that's what I'll pray for." My mother didn't offer her usual objections to talk about him actually dying and it was with a heavy heart that I drove the 86 miles home to Kennebunk, knowing I would never see my father alive again.

I was awakened three nights later from a dream — of my grandmother reaching out her hand to my father — by my mother's phone call telling me he was gone.

I didn't know it at the time, but nothing in my life would ever be the same again.